LECTIO DIVINA
WITH THE SPIRITUAL MASTERS

The Book of Daniel with St. Jerome

LECTIO DIVINA
WITH THE SPIRITUAL MASTERS

The Book of Daniel with St. Jerome

Compiled and adapted by
TAN Books

TAN Books
Gastonia, North Carolina

Lectio Divina with the Spiritual Masters: The Book of Daniel with St. Jerome uses this translation of St. Jerome's commentaries from the public domain: *Jerome's Commentary on Daniel*, translated by Gleason L. Archer, Jr., Baker Book House, 1958.

Unless otherwise noted, Scripture quotations are from the Douay-Rheims Bible, available in the Public Domain.

Compiled and adapted by TAN Books

Cover and interior design by Jordan Avery

Artwork by Chris Lewis, Baritus Catholic Illustration | barituscatholic.com

ISBN: 978-1-5051-3674-6
ePUB ISBN: 978-1-5051-4020-0

Published in the United States by
TAN Books
PO Box 269
Gastonia, NC 28053

www.TANBooks.com

Printed in the United States of America

"Read the divine Scriptures frequently; rather, may your hands never set the Holy Book down."

—St. Jerome

CONTENTS

PUBLISHER'S INTRODUCTION

What Is Lectio Divina?

Lectio Divina, which translates from Latin as "divine reading," is a traditional spiritual practice in Catholicism involving the contemplative reading of Scripture. It dates back to the early Christian monastics and was formalized in the twelfth century by a Carthusian monk named Guigo II. The process is designed to promote communion with God and to increase the knowledge of God's Word.

> "Lectio divina is a great river that carries all the riches accumulated over the course of Church history by the fervent readers of God's Word. 'Lectio divina' is never solely our own reading. It feeds on the interpretation of those who have preceded us . . . if we persevere in 'lectio divina' and silent listening to what the Spirit is saying to the Churches, our effort will be rewarded by unheard-of jewels and riches."
>
> —Cardinal Robert Sarah

Who Is a Spiritual Master?

The Spiritual Masters are those saints who have given the Church spiritual guidance applicable to all generations. The sanctity we are striving for is found in their writings and in their witness as faithful, holy Catholics. We sit at their feet, desiring to know more of this inner life of the Trintiy that began at our Baptism. We want to grow in holiness and become saints.

What Is Lectio Divina with the Spiritual Masters?

In the book of Acts, there is the story of the eunuch who encounters Philip. Philip asks the question, "Do you know what you are reading?" The eunuch responds, "How can I unless someone explains it to me?" Many times, Catholics have a similar experience when reading Sacred Scripture alone or trying to do Lectio Divina. Even faithful Catholics go through dry periods of prayer when it can even be difficult to bring themselves to intentional prayer time.

Fruitful times of prayer and fruitful Lectio Divina usually depend upon knowledge of Scripture and the strength of imaginative prayer. If these two things are lacking in prayer, we may draw very little consolation or direction from the Holy Spirit.

TAN Books has created a structured approach to the books of the Bible with enriching commentary from the spiritual masters, meditations to draw the reader into the story, and relevant prompts based on the text and the wisdom of the saint to draw the reader up and lead them to contemplation. We want Catholics to pray the Scriptures and practice Lectio Divina with the saints whose spiritual guidance is necessary for our sanctity and growth in holiness.

HOW TO USE THIS BOOK

The Steps of Lectio Divina with the Spiritual Masters

1. LECTIO—Read with the Spiritual Masters

The first step is **reading**. Read the passage of Scripture carefully, more than once if need be. You will notice **words in bold** throughout the text. This is to catch your attention because the Spiritual Master will comment on these particular passages. Next, you read the **Reading with** ___________ section, which is the commentary on that section of Scripture by the Spiritual Master. The Spiritual Master will guide your prayer of Scripture with insights that will spiritually benefit you in your call to holiness.

2. MEDITATIO—Pray with the Spiritual Masters

The second step is **meditation**. Building on the Scripture passage and commentary, use your imagination to enter into the Biblical scene in order to prayerfully consider the setting, the people, and the divine action. The meditatio section will give your mind material for meditation on both the story of salvation and the Truths of the Catholic Faith. It is through this meditation that you enter the text and discover its further meaning for you.

3.ORATIO—Pray with the Spiritual Masters

The next step is **prayer**. This is your response to the text and meditation. Through prayerful engagement with your needs and intentions, the needs and intentions of others, and the text, offer your prayers to the Trinity through the intercession of Our Lady and the Spiritual Master. The questions in this section seek to guide the reader to deeper devotion, a strengthened will, and an enlightened intellect.

4. CONTEMPLATIO—Contemplate

Contemplation is a simple gaze of the mind toward Christ and the things of God. Aided by God's grace, you are raised above meditation to a place of resting with God in Truth. Contemplation is:

"The enjoyable admiration of perceived truth."
—St. Augustine

"Elevation of the mind resting on God."
—St. Bernard of Clairvaux

"Simple intuition of divine truth that produces love."
—St. Thomas Aquinas

". . . nothing else than a close sharing between friends; it means taking time frequently to be alone with him who we know loves us."
—St. Teresa of Ávila

"When we pray, we speak to God; but when we read, God speaks to us."
—St. Jerome

THE DOUAY-RHEIMS TRANSLATION

The Douay-Rheims Bible is a scrupulously faithful translation into English of the Latin Vulgate Bible, which Saint Jerome (342–420 AD) translated into Latin *from the original languages*. The Vulgate quickly became the Bible universally used in the Latin Rite.

Saint Jerome, who was one of the four great Western Fathers of the Church, was a man raised up by God to translate the Holy Bible into the common Latin tongue of his day. He knew Latin and Greek perfectly; he also knew Hebrew and Aramaic nearly as well. He was 1500 years closer to the original languages than any scholar today, which would make him a much better judge of the exact meaning of any Greek or Hebrew word in the Scriptures. Besides being a towering linguistic genius, he was also a great saint, and he had access to ancient Hebrew and Greek manuscripts of the second and third centuries, *which have since perished and are no longer available to scholars today*. St. Jerome's translation, moreover, was a careful, word-for-word rendering of the original texts into Latin.

The Latin Vulgate Bible, from St. Jerome, has been read and honored by the Western Church for *fifteen hundred years*! It was declared by the Council of Trent to be the official Latin version of the canonical Scriptures. Hear what the Sacred Council decreed: "Moreover, the same Holy Council . . . ordains and declares that the old Latin Vulgate Edition, which, in use for so many hundred years, had been approved by the Church, be in public lectures, disputations, sermons and expositions held as authentic, and that no one dare or presume under any pretext whatsoever to reject it." (Fourth Session, April 8, 1546). As Pope Pius XII stated in his 1943 encyclical letter *Divino Afflante Spiritu*, this means the Vulgate is "free from any error whatsoever in matters of faith and morals." And the Douay-Rheims Bible is *a faithful, word-for-word translation of the Latin Vulgate Bible of St. Jerome*.

The Latin Vulgate New Testament was translated into English by members of the English College, Douai, in 1582, predating the King James Version (commissioned 1604, first published 1611). The Old Testament portion that makes up the Douay-Rheims Bible was translated into two volumes in 1609 and 1610 in Reims, France. Thus, the *Douay-Rheims* Bible.

INTRODUCTION TO THE BOOK OF DANIEL

Daniel is one of the great prophetic figures of the Old Testament. Tradition holds that he was a noble youth of Judah, taken into exile in Babylon during the reign of King Jehoiakim (c. 605 BC), and educated in the court of Nebuchadnezzar. Despite living far from his homeland, Daniel remained steadfast in his faith, honoring the God of Israel even amid the temptations, idolatry, and political intrigues of Babylonian culture. Known for his wisdom, courage, and devotion, he became a trusted advisor to successive kings, demonstrating that fidelity to God can coexist with service in secular society.

The Book of Daniel is one of the most remarkable texts of the Old Testament. Classified among the prophetic writings, it is both historical and apocalyptic, blending court narratives with visionary revelations of God's ultimate plan. The Church has long recognized Daniel's dual witness as a model of virtuous conduct and as a prophet who reveals God's sovereignty over history. While some modern scholars date parts of the book to the second century BC, during the persecution of the Jews under Antiochus IV Epiphanes, the Church reads Daniel as inspired Scripture, with Truths that transcend historical debates.

The work is divided into two main sections. The first half (Daniel 1–6) recounts narratives of Daniel and his companions—Shadrach, Meshach, and Abednego—refusing to abandon their faith, surviving trials in the Babylonian and Persian courts, and displaying God's miraculous protection. These stories, such as Daniel in the lions' den and the fiery furnace, illustrate the principle that steadfastness in faith brings divine deliverance. They are moral exemplars, encouraging the faithful to trust God even under persecution.

The second half (Daniel 7–12) is apocalyptic in nature. Daniel receives visions of beasts, kingdoms, and the coming of the "Son of Man," who will establish an everlasting dominion (Daniel 7:13–14). These visions reveal God's ultimate control over human history, the rise and fall of empires, and the triumph of His kingdom. Daniel's apocalyptic prophecies are rich in symbolic imagery, numbers, and angelic interpretation, emphasizing both the certainty of divine justice and the hope of salvation. The Church sees in these visions a prefiguration of Christ and the final resurrection, connecting the suffering of God's people with the ultimate victory of the Messiah.

From the outset, Daniel is portrayed as a model of prayer, fasting, and reliance on God. Even when the edicts of kings' conflict with divine law, he prays openly, interprets dreams by God's guidance, and acts with wisdom and courage. His life demonstrates that holiness and civic responsibility are not mutually exclusive. The narratives emphasize that true wisdom comes from God, not from earthly power, and that God's kingdom will endure beyond the mightiest empires of men.

Scholars note that the Book of Daniel reflects two distinct historical settings. The narratives likely recall Babylonian exile traditions from the sixth century BC, while the apocalyptic visions address the trials of Jews under Seleucid oppression in the second century BC. Regardless of historical composition, the Church acknowledges the Book of Daniel as inspired Scripture. His visions are not only predictions but also assurances that God remains sovereign, even when earthly powers appear supreme.

Ultimately, the Book of Daniel challenges and inspires readers to faithfulness, courage, and hope. Like Daniel, the faithful are called to witness to God's Truth in every circumstance, trusting that He governs history and that the righteous will share in His eternal kingdom. For the Church, Daniel serves as both a model of virtuous living in exile and a prophetic voice pointing to the coming of Christ, the true fulfillment of God's promises to His people.

INTRODUCTION TO SAINT JEROME

Saint Jerome, one of the greatest Fathers of the Church and a preeminent scholar of Scripture, was born as Eusebius Hieronymus Sophronius around AD 347 in the town of Stridon, located on the border of Dalmatia and Pannonia. He received an early classical education, studying grammar, rhetoric, and philosophy in Rome, where he immersed himself in Latin and Greek literature. Despite the intellectual prestige of his studies, Jerome soon turned his heart to the study of the Scriptures, recognizing that true wisdom is rooted in the knowledge of God.

After a period of youthful indulgence, Jerome experienced a profound spiritual conversion. He was baptized and committed himself to a life of asceticism, prayer, and rigorous study. He spent several years in the Syrian desert, embracing solitude, fasting, and penance, living among monks who guided him in the disciplines of contemplation and spiritual discernment. This formative period shaped his character: austere, disciplined, and unwaveringly devoted to God.

Jerome's life was defined by the pursuit of Scripture. Fluent in Hebrew, Greek, and Latin, he devoted himself to translating and interpreting the sacred texts, seeking to render them accessible to the faithful. His most enduring work, the Vulgate, remains the Church's authoritative Latin translation of the Bible, a monumental achievement that brought clarity and uniformity to Scripture for generations. Jerome's translation was not merely linguistic; it was deeply theological, carefully harmonizing fidelity to the original texts with pastoral concerns for the Church.

Beyond his scholarship, Jerome was a tireless polemicist and spiritual guide. He engaged in vigorous correspondence with bishops, monks, and Christian leaders, offering counsel on matters of doctrine, monastic discipline, and moral conduct. His letters reveal a keen intellect, a sharp tongue, and a pastoral heart, unafraid to challenge pride, laxity, or heresy. Among his most famous correspondents was Saint Paula of Rome, whom he guided in founding monasteries and cultivating lives of deep devotion.

Jerome also produced extensive commentaries on nearly every book of the Bible, combining philological precision with spiritual insight. His commentaries on Isaiah, the Psalms, and the Gospels remain seminal works of biblical exegesis. He emphasized that the study of Scripture must be both intellectual and spiritual, insisting that understanding must lead to the transformation of one's heart and life. For Jerome, knowledge without holiness was incomplete; learning served the purpose of drawing the soul closer to God.

Although he spent the majority of his life in Bethlehem, establishing a monastery and living in study and prayer, Jerome traveled widely, including stints in Rome, Antioch, and Constantinople, and sought guidance from prominent Church leaders such as Pope Damasus I. Despite his often fiery temperament and disputes with contemporaries, his zeal was always rooted in love for God and the Church.

Saint Jerome died on September 30, AD 420, in Bethlehem, where he had spent decades in monastic scholarship. His life was characterized by ascetic rigor, unyielding dedication to Scripture, and tireless pastoral care. The Church honors him as a Doctor of the Church, recognizing his profound influence on theology, biblical scholarship, and the spiritual life of Christians across the centuries.

Saint Jerome's legacy endures not only in the Vulgate but also in his example of disciplined study, courageous truth-telling, and passionate devotion to God. He demonstrates that scholarship and sanctity are not opposed but complementary, and that the life of the mind, when ordered toward God, can illuminate the faith of the entire Church.

PRAYER BEFORE READING SCRIPTURE

Prayer for Knowledge of Scripture

Lord God, let us keep your Scriptures in mind
and meditate on them day and night,
persevering in prayer, always on watch.
We beg you, Lord, to give us real knowledge of what we read,
and to show us not only how to understand it,
but how to put it into practice,
and to obtain spiritual gifts
enlightened by the teaching of the Holy Spirit,
through Jesus Christ our Lord,
whose power and glory will endure throughout all ages.
Amen.
—Origen (c. 185–254)

Prayer before Meditation

My Lord and my God, I firmly believe that you are here; that you see me, that you hear me. I adore you with profound reverence; I beg your pardon for my sins, and the grace to make this time of prayer fruitful. My Immaculate Mother, Saint Joseph my father and lord, my guardian angel, intercede for me. Amen.

Prayer to the Holy Spirit

Come, O Holy Spirit, fill the hearts and minds of your faithful servants and inflame them with the fire of your Divine love.

LET US PRAY

O God, who by the inspiration of the Holy Spirit did instruct the hearts of your faithful servants, grant us in the same Spirit to discern what is right and enjoy His comfort for ever. Through our Lord Jesus Christ, who lives and reigns one God with you and the same Spirit, world without end. Amen.

LECTIO: DANIEL 1:1–5

Subject: Theodicy, The Land of Confusion (Eccl. 8:14), Eunuchs for the Kingdom

1 In the third year of the reign of Joakim king of Juda, Nabuchodonosor king of Babylon came to Jerusalem, and besieged it. 2 **And the Lord delivered into his hands Joakim** the king of Juda, and part of the vessels of the house of God: and **he carried them away into the land of Sennaar**, to the house of his god, and the vessels he brought into the treasure house of his god. 3 And the king spoke to Asphenez the master of the eunuchs, that he should bring in some of the children of Israel, and of the king's seed and of the princes, 4 Children in whom there was no blemish, well favoured, and skillful in all wisdom, acute in knowledge, and instructed in science, and such as might stand in the king's palace, that he might teach them the learning, and the tongue of the Chaldeans. 5 And the king appointed them a daily provision, of his own meat, and of the wine of which he drank himself, that being nourished three years, afterwards they might stand before the king.

Reading with Saint Jerome

The Babylonian exile (c. 597–538 BC) was an event of immeasurable crisis for the Jewish people. It caused not only political and national disaster, but also an unmatched crisis of faith. God had promised Abraham and his descendants that they would live in this land forever, that they would be His people and He would be their God. But in 597 BC, the King of Babylon, Nubuchiudnezer, invaded Judah, destroyed Jerusalem and the Temple, and brought the survivors away with him back to the land of Babylon. The book of Daniel begins right after the Hebrew survivors have arrived in Babylon. But the Jewish people had a great question: How could such disaster happen to God's chosen people? Is God unfaithful? Is God not truly all-powerful? Saint Jerome reads Daniel closely and shows us that this exile was actually the *will of God*, and that the people had been *delivered into the hands* of the King of Babylon (Dan. 1:2). Jerome tells us, "The fact that Joakim is recorded to have been given over shows that it was not a victory for the might of his enemies but rather it was of the will of the Lord" (*Comm.* Ch. 1, v. 2).

Jerome makes the connection that this is not the first time we have encountered Babylon in the history of Gods people. It is the place where the Tower of Babel was erected (Gen. 11). He says, "From this circumstance and from the confusion of tongues the region received the name Babylon, which, translated into our language, means 'confusion'" (*Comm.* Ch. 1, v. 2).

Having been taken away from Jerusalem and the Temple seems to mean being taken away from God, but it is not abandonment. The Lord will still speak to His people through prophets even though they are exiled in a foreign land. As Daniel, Hananiah, Mishael, and Azariah were singled out for service to the King of Babylon, so God will raise them up as His witnesses and prophets even in the distant land. Jerome notes, "The Hebrews think that Daniel, Hananiah, Mishael, and Azariah were eunuchs, thus fulfilling that prophecy which is spoken by Isaiah regarding Hezekiah: 'And they shall take of thy seed and make eunuchs of them in the house of the king of Babylon' (Is. 37:7). If however they were of the seed royal, there is no doubt but what they were of the line of David" (*Comm.* Ch. 1, v. 3).

MEDITATIO

1. The Problem of Evil

The beginning of the book of Daniel thrusts us immediately into the problem of Theodicy: if God is good, why does He allow evil? Why does God let bad things happen to good people? But it is even more difficult than that: Jerome notes that God "delivered them." God Himself hands His people over into exile. But why? Why would He do this? We must first understand that God always acts for our greatest good. His ultimate goal for us is heaven. But sometimes our road has great detours along the way. The Hebrew people had been unfaithful to the covenant for centuries, and even after generations of warnings by the prophets, they still showed no signs of turning back to the Lord. So the Lord gave them what they wanted. They sought after false gods, so He handed them into their own desires. Sometimes the Lord gives us what we seek: the consequences of our sins. But we need to dig deep here. For many of us, we need to hit rock bottom before we turn back to Him. The prodigal son needed to find himself in the mud with the pigs before he turned back. Here, the people of Israel needed to live in a foreign land and literally be taken away before they would remember the Lord.

But God does not deal with us "from a distance." He did not keep our fallen state far from Him. He spanned the infinite distance and became one of us. He handed Himself over to death and went further than the furthest sinner in order to redeem us all. His rock bottom went deeper than we could ever go. Now there is no darkness, no distance where Christ has not gone before us. When we feel ourselves handed over, experiencing the effects of evil, we need only to turn to Him, for He has already walked this road before us.

2. Back to Babel. The Land of Confusion

Yet, still, we find ourselves in lands of confusion. Jerome notes that Babylon comes from Babel, meaning "land of confusion." The Hebrews are back in the place where the Lord originally scattered the people who were making the Tower of Babel. So why are they back there? Because the choice for sin is an illogical choice, and it leads to even more confusion. The people of Israel had neglected God and His law for so many centuries that the Lord now gave them fully over to the consequences of their sins, and they found themselves in the land of confusion. But that is the way it is for us, too. Sin is not only a choice against grace, but it's a choice against reason. We are choosing to abandon reason and embrace confusion. And if we are honest, we can recognize that in the frenzy of temptation a spirit of confusion takes over. When we consent to sin, we embrace a fleeting pleasure for whatever the consequences of our sin will be. It is only when we regain a sense of reason that repentance starts to draw us out of a land of confusion and back into alignment with God.

ORATIO

1. What situation in my life do I find it difficult to trust in God's providence? Do I feel like God has "delivered me" into evil? Why might this be?

2. Is there something in my life that is leading me back into confusion? The Lord brings order to the confusion of my life. Am I choosing Him continually, or do I allow myself to choose sins that lead me back into darkness?

3. Do I live my life for the kingdom of God? Do I devote myself first and foremost to His kingdom? Do I "seek first the kingdom"?

CONTEMPLATIO

LECTIO: DANIEL 1:6–16

Subject: Who Am I? Fidelity in Distress, Providence and Protection

6 Now there were among them of the children of Juda, Daniel,
Ananias, Misael, and Azarias. 7 **And the master of the eunuchs**
gave them names: to Daniel, Baltasar: to Ananias, Sidrach: to
Misael, Misach: and to Azarias, Abdenago. 8 But Daniel pur-
posed in his heart that he would not be defiled with the king's
table, nor with the wine which he drank: and he requested the
master of the eunuchs that he might not be defiled. 9 **And God**
gave to Daniel grace and mercy in the sight of the prince of the
eunuchs. 10 And the prince of the eunuchs said to Daniel: I fear
my lord the king, who hath appointed you meat and drink: who if
he should see your faces leaner than those of the other youths your
equals, you shall endanger my head to the king. 11 **And Daniel**
said to Malasar, whom the prince of the eunuchs had appoint-
ed over Daniel, Ananias, Misael, and Azarias: 12 **Try, I beseech**
thee, thy servants for ten days, and let pulse be given us to
eat, and water to drink: 13 **And look upon our faces, and the**
faces of the children that eat of the king's meat: and as thou
shalt see, deal with thy servants. 14 And when he had heard these
words, he tried them for ten days. 15 And after ten days their faces
appeared fairer and fatter than all the children that ate of the king's
meat. 16 So Malasar took their portions, and the wine that they
should drink: and he gave them pulse.

Reading with Saint Jerome

Daniel and the three young men are given new Babylonian names, Baltasar, Sidrach Misach, and Abdenago.

Jerome points out that this is not the first time names have been changed in exile (*Comm.* Ch. 1, v. 7). For Pharaoh had also changed the name of Joseph to Somtonphanec (Gen. 41) when he was in Egypt. But he sees that the Lord Himself changes names in the Bible when people are given a new mission and a new identity. "Furthermore the Lord Himself changes names benignly, and on the basis of events imposes names of special significance, so as to call Abram Abraham, and Sarai Sarah (Gen. 17). Also in the

Gospel, the former Simon received the name of Peter (Mark 3)" (*Comm.* Ch. 1, v. 7).

All the men in the service of the king were given special treatment which included eating the same food that was given to the king himself. But Daniel wanted to still be faithful to God's laws even though they were in exile and so they "preferred humble fare to royal delicacies" (*Comm.* Ch. 1, v. 9).

When the master of the eunuchs is kind to Daniel and the three young men, Jerome notes a deeper meaning than mere human kindness. He sees that all of these circumstances are in the hands of God and that He is the one still at work. Jerome says, "We may understand that if ever under pressing circumstances holy men are loved by unbelievers, it is a matter of the mercy of God, not of the goodness of perverted men" (*Comm.* Ch. 1, v. 9).

We see how Daniel's request for the humbler food shows just how great his faith was. If he was faithful to God, he believed God would take care of them. Jerome says, "He not only promised he would be in good flesh by eating the humbler food, but he even set a time-limit. Therefore, it was not a matter of temerity but of faith, for the sake of which he despised the sumptuous fare of the king" (*Comm.* Ch. 1, v. 12).

MEDITATIO

1. Who Am I?

St Jerome wants us to see the pattern here. Daniel and Joseph receive new names as foreigners in foreign lands. But the Lord gives new names when He is calling people home. He changes the names of Abram and Sarai to Abraham and Sarah when He calls them to be the beginning of His new family in the promised land. He changes Jacob's name to Israel who becomes the father of the twelve tribes. And the pattern continues in the New Testament. After his conversion, Saul is changed to Paul, and Simon is changed to Peter.

But what about us? We ask the question: who am I? How do we find out our real identity and our mission? If we look to the Gospels, we find the secret. At Caesarea Philippi, Jesus asked His apostles, "Who do you say that I am?" So Simon said, "You are the Christ, the Son of the Loving God." In response to his confession of faith Jesus said, "You are Peter and on this rock I will build my church" (Matt. 16). Simon Peter gives us the key. If we want to know who we are, we must first know who Jesus is. To find ourselves, we must first find Christ. After we come to faith in Jesus, He will reveal to us our true name and our vocation. We should stop looking at ourselves and rather look to the Lord and be radiant (Ps. 34:5).

2. Fidelity in the Midst of Distress

Again, Jerome is recognizing something deep here. Daniel's response to going into exile is faithfulness to the Lord. It wasn't even his own sins that brought him into exile, but Daniel still finds the secret of fidelity to God. Isn't he a type of Christ? He bears the burdens of the sins of others. He pays the price for sins that he did not commit. He is exiled from his homeland, and still he dedicates himself to faithfulness in the Lord. Isn't this what Jesus did for us? He left the Father's heart to go into a foreign land and pay the price for our sins, all the while bearing untiring witness to the Father's goodness. Do we really have anything to complain about? When we suffer for others' sins all we need to do is look to the cross. He is the only sinless one. If we find ourselves also hanging on a cross, then we can at least be like the good thief. Confess that we deserve it and humbly beg mercy from our crucified King.

3. Providence and Protection

St Jerome gives us another secret for the spiritual life: Everything is mercy. He notices that the kindness toward Daniel is not so much pagan virtue, but the mercy of God. We need the eyes to see that every person, every circumstance in our life, is a hidden emblem of the mercy of God. If someone is kind to us, it is Jesus in them showing love. If someone is unbearable to us, it is the Lord seeking to grow the virtue of patience in us. When a door slams in our face, it is God protecting us from something bad. He works all things for the good for those who love Him. But do we see that He is relentless in this work? Everything is protection, not rejection.

4. Not Presumption but Faith

On the surface, Daniel's boast that they will be healthier by eating the lesser food seems like presumption. But Jerome explains it is not "temerity but faith." But what is the difference between presumption and faith? The answer is subtle, yet huge. Presumption rests on us, faith rests on God. Presumption is founded on *our* belief that God will conform to our will or thinking; but faith is placing our trust in God's will, it rests solely on *Him*. But this faith comes from having a deep personal relationship with God. "Amen, amen I say to you: if you ask the Father any thing in my name, he will give it you" (John 16:23). It takes a real closeness with the Lord to make these kinds of faith-filled requests.

Think of the Syrophoenician woman or the widow begging the just judge. Even if I don't have the faith yet, I can practice it by continuing to ask. Perseverance builds up our confidence in God. We see examples of the saints doing radical things, against natural perception. But for us, we should be satisfied with the humbler food and live on faith.

ORATIO

1. Do I really know Jesus? Do I seek first the kingdom? Do I let faith be my light? Do I study my faith? Have I exposed myself to seductive errors that could lead me from the church's teaching?

2. Have I caused suffering for others because of my sins? If so, do I pray for these people? Have I suffered because of another's sins? Pray for this person and forgive them.

3. Protection, not rejection. When difficult circumstances come into my life, do I make an act of faith in Gods providence?

CONTEMPLATIO

LECTIO: DANIEL 1:17–21

Subject: Baptismal Call (Vocation), Gifts, Charisms

[17] **And to these children God gave knowledge, and understanding in every book, and wisdom: but to Daniel the understanding also of all visions and dreams.** [18] And when the days were ended, after which the king had ordered they should be brought in: the prince of the eunuchs brought them in before Nabuchodonosor. [19] And when the king had spoken to them, there were not found among them all such as Daniel, Ananias, Misael, and Azarias: and they stood in the king's presence. [20] And in all matters of wisdom and understanding, that the king inquired of them, he found them ten times better than all the diviners, and wise men, that were in all his kingdom. [21] And Daniel continued even to the first year of king Cyrus.

Reading with Saint Jerome

Jerome tells us the reason the three young men excelled in learning was not just human diligence but was because of the gift and grace of God. Their faithfulness was reciprocated by God's gift (*Comm.* Ch. 1, v. 17).

Jerome says, "Note that God is said to have given the holy lads knowledge and learning in secular literature, in every book and branch of wisdom. . . implying that they understood everything they read, and by the Spirit of God could make a judgment concerning the lore of the Chaldeans" (*Comm.* Ch. 1, v. 17).

Jerome continues, saying, "Daniel had an outstanding gift over and above the three lads, in that he could astutely discern the significance of visions and dreams in which things to come are shown forth by means of certain symbols and mysteries. Therefore that which others saw only in a shadowy appearance he could perceive clearly with the eyes of his understanding" (*Comm.* Ch. 1, v. 17). As Jerome states, these gifts come not from their own human learning, but instead show God's sovereign gift of wisdom and faithfulness to those who remain steadfast in Him, which surpasses all worldly learning and power. Through all of his trials, Daniel remained faithful to God, and God rewards him and his companions. Even in the court of this mighty king, God proves that true wisdom and enduring authority come from Him alone, not from earthly systems, and that fidelity to Him leads to lasting honor.

MEDITATIO

1. Baptismal Vocation

Daniel and his companions excelled in secular learning, yet they never lost sight of God. Whatever we do, secular or sacred, work or recreation, we should do it in the name of the Lord (Col. 3:17). As lay people, our vocation is to bring the sacred into the secular sphere, and this is done by living our daily lives for the Lord. Whether we are writers, janitors, or doctors, we should fully apply ourselves. This is what daily holiness is—living our baptismal vocation. These men were prophets, and Daniel in an extraordinary way. But by our baptism we are anointed prophets in the new kingdom of Jesus. And the way we live out this prophetic vocation is not by foretelling extraordinary future events, but rather it is by applying ourselves to our ordinary work with God's grace (*CCC* 871, 897, 1268, 1291, 1546).

2. Gifts of the Holy Spirit

God gave these men gifts of knowledge and understanding, both are gifts of the Holy Spirit. But there is a new dispensation of grace in the kingdom of Jesus. These gifts point to the gifts and charisms that Paul speaks about (see Romans 12:4–11; 1 Cor. 12:1-11; Is. 11:1–5). We usually divide these graces into two categories: charisms and the seven-fold gifts of the Holy Spirit. Each of us is given the seven gifts of the Holy Spirit at baptism and they are deepened at confirmation. But they can only be activated by the Holy Spirit. They are like sails on a sailboat. We can fly the sail, make ourselves available, but we are dependent on the wind. Only the Holy Spirit can activate these spiritual gifts. If it is God-given it must be God-directed. So how do we prepare ourselves? As St. Augustine wrote, "Work as if everything depends on us and pray as if everything depends on God." Thus is what the young men did. They studied hard but relied constantly on God for His grace and assistance, thus availing themselves to Gods gifts and direction (*CCC* 1303).

3. Charisms

Daniel had an extraordinary charism of prophecy. We too should pray about what charisms we have. Charisms are specific gifts given to each of the baptized for the building up of the Body of Christ. This requires us to constantly rely on God's grace for understanding. This is a very humble attitude that we need. We are never the owners or masters of the Word, but servants. The gifts of the Holy Spirit are primarily for our own sanctification, for the unfolding of our spiritual life. But the charisms are not for us, they are for others. They are for the building up of the Body of Christ. Not for ourselves or to be puffed up, but to be of greater service to the Body of Christ. Charisms could be extraordinary, like healing and miracles, but they can also be very ordinary, like hospitality. We should seek to know what charism(s) the Lord has given us and use it for the good of the Body of Christ (*CCC* 800, 801, 2003).

ORATIO

1. Do I do "everything in the name of the Lord"? How can I live my prophetic call better?

2. Am I daily growing in my spiritual life? Am I praying as if everything depends on God? What do I need to do to take the next step in making myself available to the Gifts of the Holy Spirit?

3. What charism has Jesus given me for the kingdom? Today, I will set aside special time to pray and ask God to show me what charisms He has given me.

CONTEMPLATIO

LECTIO: DANIEL 2:1–13

Subject: From Fear to Love

1 In **the second year** of the reign of Nabuchodonosor, Nabuchodonosor had a dream, and his spirit was terrified, and his dream went out of his mind. 2 Then the king commanded to call together the diviners and the wise men, and the magicians, and **the Chaldeans**: to declare to the king his dreams: so they came and stood before the king. 3 And the king said to them: I saw a dream: and being troubled in mind I know not what I saw. 4 And the Chaldeans answered the king in Syriac: O king, live for ever: tell to thy servants thy dream, and we will declare the interpretation thereof. 5 And the king answering said to the Chaldeans: The thing is gone out of my mind: **unless you tell me the dream, and the meaning thereof, you shall be put to death, and your houses shall be confiscated.** 6 **But if you tell the dream, and the meaning of it, you shall receive of me rewards, and gifts, and great honour:** therefore tell me the dream, and the interpretation thereof. 7 They answered again and said: Let the king tell his servants the dream, and we will declare the interpretation of it. 8 The king answered, and said: I know for certain that you seek to gain time, since you know that the thing is gone from me. 9 If therefore you tell me not the dream, there is one sentence concerning you, that you have also framed a lying interpretation, and full of deceit, to speak before me till the time pass away. Tell me therefore the dream, that I may know that you also give a true interpretation thereof. 10 Then the Chaldeans answered before the king, and said: There is no man upon earth, that can accomplish thy word, O king, neither doth any king, though great and mighty, ask such a thing of any diviner, or wise man, or Chaldean. 11 For the thing that thou askest, O king, is difficult; nor can any one be found that can shew it before the king, except the gods, whose conversation is not with men. 12 Upon hearing this, the king in fury, and in great wrath, commanded that all the wise men of Babylon should be put to death. 13 And the decree being gone forth, the wise men were slain: and Daniel and his companions were sought for, to be put to death.

Reading with Saint Jerome

King Nabuchodonosor seems to ask his counselors to perform an impossible task. He asks them not only to interpret his dream, but to tell him what he dreamt in the first place. This is certainly impossible on the natural level but not to divine grace. The king already has a sense that this dream is so important that it needs more than a mere human interpretation.

Jerome tells us that the King is using this task as a tool of discernment to see if their interpretation can be trusted. "In order that if they should be able to tell him the dream, he might therefore believe also that which was uncertain, namely the meaning of the dream. But if they should be unable to tell the king what he in his mental confusion could not recall, they would also lose claim to trustworthiness in the interpretation they might give" (*Comm.* Ch. 2, v. 5).

Jerome explains that the King "threatened punishment and offered rewards" (*Comm.* Ch. 2, v. 12) as a means of motivation. Punishment and reward is not a novel idea, but it corresponds to basic human desires, for we all wish to avoid punishment and gain rewards.

MEDITATIO

From Fear to Love

"Perfect charity casteth out fear" (1 John 4:18)

St. Jerome highlights how the king uses fear of punishment and promise of rewards as the motivation for the wisemen. But St. John tells us in his first letter that "perfect charity casteth out fear" (1 John 4:18). So is fear of punishment just a childish way of approaching religion? Should we throw out any mention of punishment and just focus on love? No . . . and yes. It is better to see the Christian life as a journey from fear to love.

The goal is perfect love, but perfect love takes a lifetime. We all start out as children in spirituality and most of us need some level of fear as a motivation. This fear of the punishment of hell is called "imperfect contrition" (*CCC* 1452, 1453). We choose the hard path to heaven for fear of the punishment of hell. It is imperfect because we are more concerned about ourselves than anything else. But a little fear of hell can go a long way. We don't want to stay in that kind of mindset, but instead we want to grow from imperfect to perfect contrition. This is sorrow for our sins not because they will bring us to hell, but because we lament at having hurt the One who has died out of love for us. We encounter the great love of Christ and now are motivated to go to heaven to be with the One we love. So fear is useful in the beginning to get us on the right track, but we want our lives to be more and more dominated by the love of Christ.

ORATIO

1. Do I realize that my sins have the real capacity to bring me to hell?

2. Am I motivated more by fear of hell or fear of losing my loving God?

3. Too much fear of hell can lead to scrupulosity. Am I scrupulous? Do I recognize that there is no sin that has not been conquered by Jesus?

CONTEMPLATIO

LECTIO: DANIEL 2: 14–19

Subject: Reliance on Grace and Prayer

14 Then Daniel inquired concerning the law and the sentence, of Ari-
och the general of the king's army, who was gone forth to kill the wise
men of Babylon. 15 And he asked him that had received the orders
of the king, why so cruel a sentence was gone forth from the face of
the king. And when Arioch had told the matter to Daniel, 16 **Daniel
went in and desired of the king, that he would give him time
to resolve the question** and declare it to the king. 17 **And he went
into his house, and told the matter to Ananias, and Misael, and
Azarias his companions:** 18 **To the end that they should ask mercy
at the face of the God of heaven concerning this secret,** and that
Daniel and his companions might not perish with the rest of the wise
men of Babylon. 19 Then was the mystery revealed to Daniel by a
vision in the night: and Daniel blessed the God of heaven.

Reading with Saint Jerome

The wise men of Babylon already admitted that they could not tell the king what his dream was but, Daniel asked to have time in order to pursue the answer. He is not stalling, nor is he looking for answers through human knowledge, but rather he begs the Lord for revelation about the mysteries. St. Jerome writes, "Daniel requested time, not that he might investigate secret things by the clever application of his intellect, but that he might beseech the Lord of Secrets" (*Comm.* Ch. 2, v. 16–17). But he did not rely on his own merit before the Lord or the power of his own prayer. This is why he asked the three young men to join in him in supplication to the Lord. St. Jerome says, "And for that reason he engaged Hananiah, Mishael, and Azariah to join with him in supplication, to avoid the appearance of presuming upon his own merit alone, and to the end that those involved in a common danger might engage in common prayer" (*Comm.* Ch. 2, v. 16–17).

MEDITATIO

The Reliance on Grace and Prayer

St. Jerome highlights two aspects of our spiritual life that at first glance seem contradictory: the reliance on grace, and the power of common prayer. But if we look closer, we can see that they go perfectly together. In fact, the one leads to the other. Grace aligns us with God and His ways, and after that we are ready to ask with great boldness. Let us look at each one briefly.

1. Reliance on Grace

First, St. Jerome notes that Daniel did not rely on human ingenuity but sought the Lord's grace and revelation in order to understand the spiritual vision. We have no ability to uncover God's secrets by our own efforts. We cannot approach Him like Prometheus who stole fire from the gods and gave it to man. We can only enter by His grace and permission. We need to call this to mind whenever we read scripture—we are never the masters of the Word but always servants of the Word.

At the last supper Jesus told His disciples, "Without me you can do nothing" (John 15:5), and He was not exaggerating. He did not say 'Without me you can do a little bit' or 'Without me you can do some things.' No, without Him we can do *nothing*. From our very being we are in total dependence on Him. Right now, this minute, our very existence is dependent on Him. If He stopped thinking about us for one second we would just cease to exist. Even more so in our spiritual lives. We are utterly dependent on His grace. Grace is the beginning, middle, and completion of any good work. We cannot work our way to heaven as the Pelagian heresy taught. We need His grace. This is not a call to a purely passive kind of spiritual life. No! We must cooperate actively with God. But we should call to mind over and over that even our desire to pray is a response to this movement of grace.

Everything we do in our spiritual life is a response to the work He has already done. When we choose to pray, this is because He has already tugged on our hearts with His grace. When we do some good work, we are responding to the movement of charity the Holy Spirit is already working in us. So our spiritual life truly is grace. As St. Therese said, "Everything is a grace."

2. **Prayer in Common**

All of our prayer as Christians is prayer in common. Even hermits do not pray in isolation. We are united as one in the Body of Christ. The prayer Jesus Himself taught us reminds us of this when we pray "*Our* Father." So the Christian life is a life in communion with others. But the Lord also counsels us on the power of common prayer. He says, "Again I say to you, that if two of you shall consent upon earth, concerning any thing whatsoever they shall ask, it shall be done to them by my Father who is in heaven.

For where there are two or three gathered together in my name, there am I in the midst of them" (Mt. 18:19–20).

Do we realize the power He has placed in our hands? He wants us to ask—not in isolation, but to join our intentions together. If we need an example we have to look only at the apostles after the Ascension of Jesus. They joined together with Mary in the upper room and prayed fervently for nine days. They were completely united in imploring God's direction, and the result of this joint prayer was the coming of the Holy Spirit at Pentecost. What if we prayed like that? What could happen in our lives and in the Church if we prayed together with that kind of fervor?

ORATIO

1. Do I ask for God's grace and direction in prayer? Or do I have my own agenda in prayer? Am I asking that *His* will be done or *my* will be done?

2. Do I see that my prayer affects the whole Body of Christ? What intentions do I need to join with others in praying for?

CONTEMPLATIO

LECTIO: DANIEL 2:20–23

Subject: Deep Prayer and Dark Prayer

20 And speaking he said: **Blessed be the name of the Lord from
eternity and for evermore: for wisdom and fortitude are
his.** 21 And he changeth times and ages: taketh away kingdoms
and establisheth them, giveth wisdom to the wise, and knowledge
to them that have understanding. 22 **He revealeth deep and hid-
den things, and knoweth what is in darkness: and light is with
him.** 23 To thee, O God of our fathers, I give thanks, and I praise
thee: because thou hast given me wisdom and strength: and now
thou hast shewn me what we desired of thee, for thou hast made
known to us, the king's discourse.

Reading with Saint Jerome

Daniel's confidence in approaching the Lord comes from his deep abiding awareness of the Lord's Presence. He is already in a profound relationship with the Lord, and that is why he can ask God for the kind of revelation that he seeks. St. Jerome highlights Daniel as a man of deep prayer, saying, "A man to whom God makes profound revelations . . . he it is who by the indwelling Spirit probes even into the deep things of God, and digs the deepest of wells in the depths of his soul. He is a man who has stirred up the whole earth, which is wont to conceal the deep waters, and he observes the command of God, saying: 'Drink water from thy vessels and from the spring of thy wells' (Prov. 5:15)" (*Comm.* Ch. 2, v. 22).

There is a paradox regarding the prayer of Daniel when he says the Lord " knoweth what is in darkness." We usually think of God in regard to light, and the dark as what is opposed to God. But St. Jerome notes that the scriptures reveal this kind of framework as a shallow assessment of things. There is in fact a more mature way to understand that there is indeed a kind of "darkness" in God. Regarding this darkness, Jerome says, "We should interpret the words to mean all the dark mysteries and deep things (concerning God), according to what we read in Proverbs: "He understands also the parable and the dark saying." This in turn is equivalent to what we read in the Psalms: 'Dark waters in the clouds of the sky' (Ps. 17:12)" (*Comm.* Ch. 2, v. 22).

The one who becomes familiar with God begins to experience God's mystery, and from this place of darkness can communicate these mysteries to others. Jerome says this is what Daniel is in this scene. "For one who ascends to the heights and forsakes the things of earth, and like the birds themselves seeks after the most rarified atmosphere and everything ethereal, he becomes like a cloud to which the truth of God penetrates and which habitually showers rain upon the saints. Replete with a plenitude of knowledge, he contains in his breast many dark waters enveloped with deep darkness, a darkness which only Moses can penetrate (Ex. 23) and speak with God face to face, of Whom the Scripture says: 'He hath made darkness His hiding-place' (Ps. 17:12)" (*Comm.* Ch. 2, v. 22).

MEDITATIO

St. Jerome again highlights two contours of prayer that are essential for us to grow in our spiritual life: deep prayer and prayer in darkness.

1. Deep Prayer

"Launch out into the deep" (Luke 5:4).

It is important for us to realize that deep prayer is not just for monks and nuns. It is part of the call of each Christian. In the year 2000, Pope St. John Paul II encouraged the whole Church to *Duc in altum*, "Launch out into the deep." (Luke 5:4). He called every member of the faithful not to be satisfied with a shallow prayer life but to put out into the deep waters of prayer. We need this more than ever. Our lives have become so fractured that we need to set aside real time, actual time, to grow in our relationship with Jesus. This may start out as just a few little prayers a day, but we mustn't be satisfied with a little. God has so much to offer us. We must stir up in ourselves a desire to not be satisfied with a shallow prayer life. St. John of the Cross said, "We must then dig deeply in Christ. He is like a rich mine with many pockets containing treasures: however deep we dig we will never find their end or their limit. Indeed, in every pocket new seams of fresh riches are discovered on all sides" (cf. Office of Readings, Spiritual Canticle).

2. Dark Prayer

But if we persevere in deep prayer we will come, sooner or later, into the prayer of darkness.

Now, St. Jerome highlights the strangeness that scripture uses both light and darkness when speaking of God. So, how can we make sense of this? We say in the Creed that the Son of God is Light from Light. For, "God is light, and in Him there is no darkness" (1 John 1:5). It is more proper to say that as we encounter this pure light, our *experience* is darkness. Just as our natural eyes cannot look directly at the sun, even more so our spiritual eyes cannot handle the pure light of God. So our experience as we encounter the pure light of God is like being blinded by the light. We walk by faith, not by sight.

There can be extreme forms of this darkness, such as the dark night of the soul, but even if we do not experience this advanced state, we will still experience times of dryness, lack of feeling, etc. . . . Such times are incredibly important. For just as roots grow deeper when it is dry, so too our faith becomes firmer if we persevere in prayer during times of darkness.

But why does the Lord bring about times of darkness? Sooner or later we must face up to how selfish we really are. We tend to be more attached to His gifts of peace and tasting the sweetness of His friendship than truly attached to *Him*. We are more in love with the gifts than with the Giver. He wants our love for Him to grow firm. He wants us to grow from children into friends and even lovers. In order to do this, He begins to remove that childish food of sweetness, and gives us the mature food of dryness and darkness. We do not need to seek out these times, however. Just seek Him. Let Him be in charge of our path. Let Him be our guide.

St. John of the Cross can again be our teacher in these times. When darkness is felt and no light seems to show us how to move forward in prayer, it is the fire of faith and charity burning in our hearts that will guide us. (cf. "Dark Night of the Soul" by St. John of the Cross.)

ORATIO

1. What is my commitment to prayer? Do I set aside dedicated time every day to grow in deep prayer?

2. Have I experienced times of darkness in prayer? If so, what was my response? Did I abandon my prayer life when I felt no consolation or have I persevered even in dryness?

CONTEMPLATIO

LECTIO: DANIEL 2:24–30

Subject: Love of Enemies and Discernment of Spirits

24 After this Daniel went in to Arioch, to whom the king had
given orders to destroy the wise men of Babylon, and he spoke
thus to him: Destroy not the wise men of Babylon: bring me in
before the king, and I will tell the solution to the king. 25 Then
Arioch in haste brought in Daniel to the king, and said to him: I
have found a man of the children of the captivity of Juda, that will
resolve the question to the king. 26 The king answered, and said
to Daniel, whose name was Baltasar: Thinkest thou indeed that
thou canst tell me the dream that I saw, and the interpretation
thereof? 27 And Daniel made answer before the king, and said: The
secret that the king desireth to know, none of the wise men, or the
philosophers, or the diviners, or the soothsayers can declare to the
king. 28 But there is a God in heaven that revealeth mysteries, who
hath shewn to thee, O king Nabuchodonosor, what is to come to
pass in the latter times. Thy dream, and the visions of thy head
upon thy bed, are these: 29 Thou, O king, didst begin to think in
thy bed, what should come to pass hereafter: and he that revealeth
mysteries shewed thee what shall come to pass. 30 **To me also this
secret is revealed, not by any wisdom that I have more than all
men alive: but that the interpretation might be made manifest
to the king, and thou mightest know the thoughts of thy mind.**

Reading with Saint Jerome

St. Jerome begins his commentary on this passage, calling to mind the flaws of human thinking. He tells us, "The king had imagined that cleverness of the human intellect could embrace a knowledge of the future, and for that reason he had ordered the wise men of Babylon to be slain." (*Comm.* Ch. 2, v. 30).

The king had not yet understood the great difference between human ingenuity and divine revelation. His concept of religion seemed to be of a Promethean bent. In Greek myth, Prometheus stole fire from the gods and gave it to man. And the king thought if the wise men just worked harder in their religious pursuits, they could find out divine mysteries. But "dreams in which any coming events are signified and in which truth is shown forth, as it were, through a cloud, are not manifest to the conjectures or dominion of the human mind but to the knowledge of God alone" (*Comm.* Ch. 2, v. 30).

But Daniel knew that man cannot know the ways of God unless God reveals them to him. Thus Daniel interceded with the King to have mercy toward the Chaldean wise men. Jerome says, "Daniel therefore makes excuse for those who were unable to speak, and himself avoids the envy of others, lest any should imagine that he had said any of the things he was going to say by virtue of his personal wisdom" (*Comm.* Ch. 2, v. 30).

MEDITATIO

St. Jerome points us toward two fruits of deep prayer in our life: love of enemies and discernment of spirits.

1. Love of Enemies

Daniel makes excuses for the sins of others. This immediately makes us think of Jesus on the cross when He makes excuses for those who crucified Him, "Father, forgive them, for they know not what they do" (Lk. 23:34). This is comfortable when we think merely of Jesus 2000 years ago forgiving people we don't know. But it gets extremely uncomfortable when we realize that to become His disciples, we must do the same. In fact, this is not a suggestion but a requirement of following Jesus.

We are confronted here with maybe the most difficult doctrine of Christ: love of enemies. If we are really honest with ourselves there is nothing about this that we like.

It is uncomfortable when we realize that in order to call ourselves Christians we must follow His example. The Master teaches us, "Love your enemies: do good to them that hate you: and pray for them that persecute and calumniate you" (Mt. 5:44).

He commands you to forgive the person who hates you. Not just the person who annoys you, but the person who knowingly is doing you great harm. The person who intentionally is trying to kill your reputation. This is the person that Jesus says we should love and pray for. This is seemingly an impossible teaching, but it is non-negotiable. In fact, He even put it into the "Our Father" so that we say every single time, "Forgive us our trespasses as we forgive those who trespass against us." So how are we doing in forgiving those who trespass against us? "For if you will forgive men their offences, your heavenly Father will forgive you also your offences. But if you will not forgive men, neither will your Father forgive you your offences" (Mt. 6:14–15).

2. Discernment of spirits

St. Jerome highlights another fruit of familiarity with the divine presence: discernment of spirits. St. John teaches us, "Dearly beloved, believe not every spirit, but try the spirits if they be of God: because many false prophets are gone out into the world" (1 John 4:1). There is a lesson here about how to interpret images, visions, and inspirations that we might get whether in prayer or even in dreams. The first thing we need to know firmly is that no private revelation can be from God if it contradicts the public revelation guarded by the Church through the deposit of faith.

St. John of the Cross gives us practical advice if we receive inspiration or visions in prayer. These inspirations can come from three sources: the human spirit (ourselves), the diabolic spirit, or the Holy Spirit. We should not spend time worrying too much about whether something is from us or the devil. Either way, it is not from God. If God wants us to do something He will keep sending us the same inspiration over and over again. He will make it abundantly clear. The human and demonic both fatigue easily, and these inspirations will fade away. But if God wants something then he will continue with deliberate persistence. So St. John of the Cross's first method of discernment is to reject these inspirations when they come. If it is not from God, the inspirations will fade. But if it is from God, He will send them repeatedly and then we might take them more seriously, much like Daniel. At that point we should find a trusted spiritual director to help guide us. Then they can help us know whether this inspiration is just for ourselves or requires a broader response.

ORATIO

1. Has deep prayer actually had an effect on my soul? Has it brought me close to Christ in a way that has transformed my affections to be like His? Do I make excuses for those who intentionally hurt me?

2. Have I learned to recognize the presence of God? Am I familiar with Him? When inspiration comes, do I pray about it through discernment?

CONTEMPLATIO

LECTIO: DANIEL 2:31–43

Subject: Vainglory, Life as a Pilgrimage

31 Thou, O king, sawest, and behold there was as it were a great statue: this statue, which was great and high, tall of stature, stood before thee, and the look thereof was terrible. 32 The head of this statue was of fine gold, but the breast and the arms of silver, and the belly and the thighs of brass: 33 And the legs of iron, the feet part of iron and part of clay. 34 Thus thou sawest, till a stone was cut out of a mountain without hands: and it struck the statue upon the feet thereof that were of iron and of clay, and broke them in pieces. 35 Then was the iron, the clay, the brass, the silver, and the gold broken to pieces together, and became like the chaff of a summer's thrashingfloor, and they were carried away by the wind: and there was no place found for them: but the stone that struck the statue, became a great mountain, and filled the whole earth. 36 This is the dream: we will also tell the interpretation thereof before thee, O king. 37 Thou art a king of kings: and the God of heaven hath given thee a kingdom, and strength, and power, and glory: 38 And all places wherein the children of men, and the beasts of the field do dwell: he hath also given the birds of the air into thy hand, and hath put all things under thy power: thou therefore art the head of gold. 39 And after thee shall rise up **another kingdom**, inferior to thee, of silver: and another **third kingdom** of brass, which shall rule over all the world. 40 And **the fourth kingdom** shall be as iron. As iron breaketh into pieces, and subdueth all things, so shall that break and destroy all these. 41 And whereas thou sawest the feet, and the toes, part of potter's clay, and part of iron: the kingdom shall be divided, but yet it shall take its origin from the iron, according as thou sawest the iron mixed with the miry clay. 42 And as the toes of the feet were part of iron, and part of clay, the kingdom shall be partly strong, and partly broken. 43 And whereas thou sawest the iron mixed with miry clay, they shall be mingled indeed together with the seed of man, but they shall not stick fast one to another, as iron cannot be mixed with clay.

Reading with Saint Jerome

Daniel explains that the king's dream is a prophetic vision of the unfolding of consecutive kingdoms up until the coming of the Kingdom that will not be destroyed—the Kingdom of God. It is important to know that this dream and interpretation took place around 600 BC, many decades before any fulfillment of its elements.

The first Kingdom is the Babylonian empire (c. 612–539 BC) This first kingdom represented by the head of gold is that of King Neduchidnezer himself. Jerome explains, "'The head of gold . . . is thou, O king.' By this statement it is clear that the first empire, the Babylonian, is compared to the most precious metal, gold" (*Comm.* Ch. 2, v. 31).

The second kingdom (c.539–331 BC) is "the empire of the Medes and Persians, which bears a resemblance to silver, being inferior to the preceding empire, and superior to that which is to follow" (*Comm.* Ch. 2, v. 39). (We will encounter this kingdom later in Daniel as Darius and Cyrus conquer Babylon, Dan. 5:27–7:1.)

Then will arise a "third kingdom of brass, which shall rule over all the world" (c. 331–63 BC). St. Jerome tells us: "This signifies the Alexandrian empire, and that of the Macedonians, and of Alexander's successors. Now this is properly termed brazen, for among all the metals bronze possesses an outstanding resonance and a clear ring, and the blast of a brazen trumpet is heard far and wide . . ." (*Comm.* Ch. 2, v. 39). The prophecy that this third Bronze kingdom will reign over the whole known world came true with great swiftness when Alexander the Great conquered the world by the young age of thirty-three.

St. Jerome says, "Now the fourth empire, which clearly refers to the Romans, is the iron empire which breaks in pieces and overcomes all others. But its feet and toes are partly of iron and partly of earthenware, a fact most clearly demonstrated at the present time" (*Comm.* Ch. 2, v. 40). St. Jerome lived at the end of the 4th century and witnessed how fragile the Roman Empire was (c.63 BC–AD 476). In hindsight we see that it took centuries to fall. It was more of a slow crumble than a single cataclysmic event, but St. Jerome was living during very tumultuous times in the Roman Empire. "For just as there was at the first nothing stronger or hardier than the Roman realm, so also in these last days there is nothing more feeble, since we require the assistance of barbarian tribes both in our civil wars and against foreign nations" (*Comm.* Ch. 2, v. 40).

MEDITATIO

The literal meaning of Daniel's interpretation gives a clear outline of Dynastic history from Nebuchadnezzar through the Medes, Persians, Greeks, and Romans, down to the coming of Christ. This literal meaning is good for us to know because it strengthens our faith in scripture. It shows us how God has been planning for the coming of the Messiah for a long, long time. This is good for us to know historically, but there is a lesson that St. Jerome begins to open up for our particular situation in our daily life—that is, vainglory.

1. Vainglory

St. Jerome says it is appropriate that Alexander the Great's kingdom was labeled bronze or *brazen*. A little knowledge of his situation opens up precisely the reality of vainglory. Alexander was the pupil of Aristotle, the greatest of the Ancient Greek philosophers. He was only thirty-three years old when he conquered the whole known world. But then he died, and his kingdom was divided up among his generals. He had the whole world, yet he could not take any of it with him when he died.

Alexander the Great's accomplishments remind us clearly of the Lord's warning, "For what doth it profit a man, if he gain the whole world, and suffer the loss of his own soul? Or what exchange shall a man give for his soul?" (Mt. 16:26).

Alexander did actually gain the whole world, but then died just as quickly. This is a caution for us not to be "brazen" about our earthly accomplishments because they cannot be taken with us through the journey of death. No matter how great our accomplishments here, we need to "lay up to yourselves treasures in heaven: where neither the rust nor moth doth consume, and where thieves do not break through, nor steal" (Mt. 6:20).

2. Life as a Pilgrimage

St. Jerome lived at the demise of the Roman Empire. He died in 420 AD. The former glory of Rome was slowly crumbling around him throughout his life. "For we have not here a lasting city, but we seek one that is to come" (Heb. 13:14), for we are pilgrims in this life (1 Ptr. 2:11), and we need to keep our eyes fixed on the goal of eternity and run in order to win (1 Cor. 9:24).

Just as St. Jerome witnessed the collapse of the Roman Empire, we too are living in liquid modernity that is changing so quickly we can barely keep up. We should not neglect the world we live in, but we must hold onto it loosely. We must have one eye on earth and one on heaven.

ORATIO

1. Do I seek my own glory in my work, or the glory of God?

2. What kind of attachments do I have in this life? What am I holding onto that I have not given over to God?

3. Do I live every day realizing that heaven is my home? Or do I live like a practical atheist, living my days according to my own agenda?

CONTEMPLATIO

LECTIO: DANIEL 2:44–49

Subject: The Crushing Rock, Eucharistic Living, Providence of God

44 But in the days of those kingdoms the God of heaven will set up **a kingdom** that shall never be destroyed, and his kingdom shall not be delivered up to another people, and it shall break in pieces, and shall consume all these kingdoms, and itself shall stand for ever. 45 According as thou sawest that the stone was cut out of the mountain without hands, and broke in pieces, the clay, and the iron, and the brass, and the silver, and the gold, the great God hath shewn the king what shall come to pass hereafter, and the dream is true, and the interpretation thereof is faithful. 46 **Then king Nabuchodonosor fell on his face, and worshipped Daniel, and commanded that they should offer in sacrifice to him victims and incense.** 47 **And the king spoke to Daniel, and said: Verily your God is the God of gods, and Lord of kings, and a revealer of hidden things: seeing thou couldst discover this secret.** 48 Then the king advanced Daniel to a high station, and gave him many and great gifts: and he made him governor over all the provinces of Babylon, and chief of the magistrates over all the wise men of Babylon. 49 And Daniel requested of the king, and he appointed Sidrach, Misach, and Abdenago over the works of the province of Babylon: but Daniel himself was in the king's palace.

Reading with Saint Jerome

In the king's dream, the four kingdoms of gold, silver, bronze, and iron are succeeded by one final kingdom made of rock. On the surface, a rock may seem of less value than precious metals, but it is actually far more valuable. The four kingdoms are all of human origin, just as metals are forged and fashioned by man. So these kingdoms were all shaped by man. But the final kingdom of rock is made not by man, but by the hand of God. And this rock is not just an idea, but a person: Jesus Christ. St. Jerome says, "At the final period of all these empires of gold and silver and bronze and iron, a rock (namely, the Lord and Savior) was cut off without hands, that is, without copulation or human seed and by birth from a virgin's womb; and after all the empires had been crushed,

He became a great mountain and filled the whole earth" (*Comm.* Ch. 2, v. 40).

After Daniel tells the king the dream and its interpretation, the king is so grateful that he elevates him to great leadership in the kingdom. We now see God's Providence at work. Although God's people were taken by a foreign king to a foreign land, He still continues to care for them and bless them. St. Jerome explains, "It was for this very purpose that the king had beheld the dream and that the secrets of its interpretation were revealed by a mere lad, that Daniel might increase in importance and that in the place of captivity he might become ruler over all the Chaldeans, to the end that the omnipotence of God might be made known. We read that this same thing happened in the case of Joseph at the court of Pharaoh and in Egypt (Gen. 41), and also in the case of Mordecai at the court of Ahasuerus (Esth. 8). The purpose was that the Jews, as captives and sojourners in each of these nations, might receive encouragement as they beheld men of their own nation constituted as governors over the Egyptians or the Chaldeans" (*Comm.* Ch. 2, v. 48).

MEDITATIO

1. The Crushing Rock

The stone that crushes all the other kingdoms points to God establishing the Kingdom of God on earth. It comes from heaven and crushes the glory of all earthly kingdoms. But it is also a sign for us. All of our human efforts can be crushed by God. If we act like the builders of the Tower of Babel then God will come in like a wrecking ball. He has to destroy the little kingdoms that we have set up for ourselves in order to establish His kingdom in our souls. We may try to resist and hold on tightly to our pathetic kingdoms, but resistance is futile. St. Mother Teresa used to say, "If you want to make God laugh, tell Him your plans."

2. Eucharistic Living

But the Rock not made by hands also points to God's direct intervention in the virgin birth. No human effort could ever achieve this divine work. In fact, this prophecy shows us clearly what divine work actually is.

In the bread of life discourse, as Jesus is unfolding the mystery of the Eucharist, He was asked, "What shall we do, that we may work the works of God? Jesus answered, and said to them: This is the work of God, that you believe in him whom he hath sent" (John 6:28–29).

Jesus was asked how a person could do the work of God. And he said, "You can't do the work of God, it's the work *of God*. Only God can do God's work." Our job is to "believe in the one He sent." The only way we can approach participating in His work is through faith. Faith in Jesus is the key that opens up even our possibility of doing the work of God.

This divine work of the Eucharist is emphasized at the beginning of the Eastern liturgy. After preparing the elements for the liturgy, the deacon says to the priest, "Father, let us go, it is time for the Lord to act." This is because in the liturgy it is really Jesus who works the miracle of the Eucharist. The priest lends his body and mind to Jesus as His instrument, but it is truly Jesus who does the work.

And we can have this Eucharistic attitude in our daily life. We can be the deacon, or "servant" of our day. When we rise, we can lay the elements of our day—the meetings, computer work, phone calls, house cleaning—before the Lord and say to ourselves, "Come it is time for the Lord to act." Then we work with a Eucharistic mindset, always asking Jesus to be the main worker doing the work of God through our work.

3. The Providence of God

We come again to the mystery of God's Providence. St. Jerome wants us to see that there is no situation or circumstance that is outside of God's wisdom. If we can see this pattern in the history of Israel from Joseph to Mordecai and Daniel, then we will be able to see it in our lives. It is not just history, but mystery. It is not just in the history of Israel, but it is in the mystery of our lives. Whether we are in a monastery, an office building, or a jail cell, there is no circumstance that is outside of God's providence. If we simply turn to Him and offer our present situation to Him, He will be there to help. He is already there, in fact. In some mysterious way He has already led us there. Even if it is our sins that have brought us to the current issue. In a radically mysterious way, God is still at work. It is not that He has willed us to sin, but "where sin abounded, grace did more abound" (Rom. 5:20b). All that is needed is for us to turn to Him now and offer Him our entire life: past, present, and future.

We should not spend time saying, "If only . . . If only I was a monk and had time I would pray," "If only I had money I could be generous . . ." Daniel did not say "If only I weren't a slave," he just did the work God gave him and he was raised up.

St. Maximilian Kolbe and St. Edith Stein became saints at Auschwitz under the worst possible conditions. Every situation is at God's disposal if we allow Him to work.

ORATIO

1. What little kingdoms am I holding onto for myself? Are there situations in my life that God needs to "crush" in order to establish His kingdom in my life?

2. How can I cultivate a Eucharistic mindset for my life?

3. Do I believe that God is really at work? That He really has my life in His hands?

CONTEMPLATIO

LECTIO: DANIEL 3:1–8

Subject: Spirituality of Memory, Heresy and humility, Envy.

1 **King Nabuchodonosor made a statue of gold, of sixty cubits high, and six cubits broad, and he set it up in the plain of Dura of the province of Babylon.** 2 Then Nabuchodonosor the king sent to call together the nobles, the magistrates, and the judges, the captains, the rulers, and governors, and all the chief men of the provinces, to come to the dedication of the statue which king Nabuchodonosor had set up. 3 Then the nobles, the magistrates, and the judges, the captains, and rulers, and the great men that were placed in authority, and all the princes of the provinces, were gathered together to come to the dedication of the statue, which king Nabuchodonosor had set up. And they stood before the statue which king Nabuchodonosor had set up. 4 **Then a herald cried with a strong voice: To you it is commanded, O nations, tribes, and languages:** 5 **That in the hour that you shall hear the sound of the trumpet, and of the flute, and of the harp, of the sackbut, and of the psaltery, and of the symphony, and of all kind of music; ye fall down and adore the golden statue which king Nabuchodonosor hath set up.** 6 But if any man shall not fall down and adore, he shall the same hour be cast into a furnace of burning fire. 7 Upon this therefore, at the time when all the people heard the sound of the trumpet, the flute, and the harp, of the sackbut, and the psaltery, of the symphony, and of all kind of music: all the nations, tribes, and languages fell down and adored the golden statue which king Nabuchodonosor had set up. 8 And presently at that very time some Chaldeans came and accused the Jews.

Reading with Saint Jerome

In the last chapter, the king encountered God's power and glory when Daniel interpreted the king's dream. But he forgets God so quickly and turns to idol worship. St. Jerome says, "How soon he forgot the truth, when he had just been worshipping a servant of God as if he had been God Himself, but now commanded a statue to be made for himself" (*Comm.* Ch. 3, v. 1).

St. Jerome sees the golden statue as a kind of sign of what heretics do in creating false doctrines. He writes, "All heretics who devise a false doctrine with the brilliance of worldly eloquence, fashion thereby a golden statue, and to the best of their ability constrain men by their persuasiveness to fall down and adore the idol of deceit" (*Comm.* Ch. 3, v. 4–5).

St. Jerome shows how the cause of the Chaldeans' accusation against the Jews was envy. "They were envious of these Jews because they had been in charge of the king's business in Babylon, and also they were offended by their foreign religion and aversion towards idols. They therefore find a pretext for accusing them to the king" (*Comm.* Ch. 3, v. 8).

MEDITATIO

1. Spirituality of Memory

How quickly the king forgot the lesson just learned in the previous chapter. But the Chosen people were not any different. Think of the golden calf: God had just saved the Israelites from slavery in Egypt through incredible signs and wonders. He parted the Red Sea and saved them. Very quickly, they arrived at Mt. Sinai, and as God revealed His law to Moses on the mountaintop, the people made a golden calf to worship. At the *same moment* He is revealing His word in such a magnificent way, they are turning to worship a false idol. And are we really any different? When we sin, isn't this because we have forgotten about God? In that moment we have forgotten, or have chosen to forget, Jesus's love for us.

It is part of our fallen nature to fall into idol worship. We are easily attracted and distracted by other lovers. The Old Testament equates idolatry with adultery. The people of Israel choose to worship another god and to neglect their true Bridegroom, choosing instead a paramour. But again, are we really any different? We taste His sweetness in prayer. We feel the extravagance of His mercy in confession. And we consume His sacred flesh in the Eucharist. But we are still attracted to sin. This is because we have spiritual amnesia. We need to develop a spirituality of memory, calling to mind throughout the day the good things the Lord has done for us.

2. Heresy and Idol Worship

At first glance, St. Jerome's insight about heretics seems esoteric, but he is giving us important guidance in our pursuit of faith. First, we should always remember that God is a mystery. The word "mystery" comes from the Greek verb *muein* which means "to behold with mouth closed." When we approach God in prayer we should always approach in humility. We should seek to be formed by the Church's faith, and trust the guidance of the saints and the Holy Spirit. We may find certain aspects of the faith difficult to believe, but it is critical for us to develop the humility to trust the Church's teaching, even though we might personally find something difficult.

3. Envy

It's not surprising that the forgetfulness of God (which leads to idol worship) creates fertile ground for sin. And in this case, it is envy.

If we have eyes to see, we can recognize the demonic quality of all this. In the mystery of the Devil's fall, there seems to have been some desire to draw worship away from God and toward himself. This caused St. Michael to rise up and declare, "Who is like God?" After Satan is cast out, he is jealous of God's love for man, and seduces man to turn toward the diabolic path, for "By the envy of the devil, death came into the world: And they follow him that are of his side" (Wis. 2:24–25).

Envy leads to death. It fosters the desire for another's death. Think of the brothers of Joseph who wanted to kill him out of jealousy. We need to be on guard for envy. It is a vicious tool Satan uses—in fact, it is demonic in origin. This is why it is so dangerous to allow envy to fester in our hearts. We need to confess it honestly to root it out completely.

ORATIO

1. How can I foster a spirituality of memory in my day? Do I thank God every day for the graces He has given me?

2. Do I study my faith? Do I make study an important part of my faith life?

3. Have I confessed the sin of envy? Do I feel envy toward another in my life?

CONTEMPLATIO

LECTIO: DANIEL 3:8–23

Subject: God is Victorious, What's the Big Deal?, Watching Our Emotions

8 And presently at that very time some Chaldeans came and ac-
cused the Jews, 9 And said to king Nabuchodonosor: O king, live
for ever: 10 Thou, O king, hast made a decree that every man that
shall hear the sound of the trumpet, the flute, and the harp, of
the sackbut, and the psaltery, of the symphony, and of all kind of
music, shall prostrate himself, and adore the golden statue: 11 And
that if any man shall not fall down and adore, he should be cast
into a furnace of burning fire. 12 Now there are certain Jews whom
thou hast set over the works of the province of Babylon, Sidrach,
Misach, and Abdenago: these men, O king, have slighted thy
decree: they worship not thy gods, nor do they adore the gold-
en statue which thou hast set up. 13 Then Nabuchodonosor in
fury, and in wrath, commanded that Sidrach, Misach, and Abde-
nago should be brought: who immediately were brought before
the king. 14 And Nabuchodonosor the king spoke to them, and
said: Is it true, O Sidrach, Misach, and Abdenago, that you do
not worship my gods, nor adore the golden statue that I have set
up? 15 Now therefore if you be ready at what hour soever you shall
hear the sound of the trumpet, flute, harp, sackbut, and psaltery,
and symphony, and of all kind of music, prostrate yourselves, and
adore the statue which I have made: but if you do not adore, you
shall be cast the same hour into the furnace of burning fire: and
who is the God that shall deliver you out of my hand? 16 **Sidrach,
Misach, and Abdenago answered and said to king Nabucho-
donosor: We have no occasion to answer thee concerning this
matter.** 17 **For behold our God, whom we worship, is able to
save us from the furnace of burning fire, and to deliver us out
of thy hands, O king.** 18 **But if he will not, be it known to thee,
O king, that we will not worship thy gods, nor adore the gold-
en statue which thou hast set up.** 19 Then was Nabuchodono-
sor filled with fury: and the countenance of his face was changed
against Sidrach, Misach, and Abdenago, and he commanded that
the furnace should be heated seven times more than it had been
accustomed to be heated. 20 And he commanded the strongest
men that were in his army, to bind the feet of Sidrach, Misach,

and Abdenago, and to cast them into the furnace of burning
fire. [21] And immediately these men were bound and were cast into
the furnace of burning fire, with their coats, and their caps, and
their shoes, and their garments. [22] **For the king's commandment
was urgent, and the furnace was heated exceedingly. And the
flame of the fire slew those men that had cast in Sidrach, Mi-
sach, and Abdenago.** [23] **But these three men, that is, Sidrach,
Misach, and Abdenago, fell down bound in the midst of the
furnace of burning fire.**

Reading with Saint Jerome

St. Jerome notes something very precise about the young men's act of faith. They do not say that God *will be* victorious but that He *is* victorious right now. Even in the midst of the threat of death by fire, they proclaim God's victory. Jerome writes, "Nor do they speak of deliverance as delayed to the distant future, but rather they promise themselves immediate succor" (*Comm.* Ch. 3, v. 17).

In St. Jerome's day, there was still pagan idol worship. Although the Christians were not overtly persecuted as they had been previously, there was still peer pressure to offer incense to idols. But St. Jerome explains, "Those who reverence God are not to worship it. Therefore let judges and princes who worship the statues of emperors or idols realize that they are doing precisely the thing which the three youths refused to do and thereby pleased God." Because, "worshipping the mere image is equivalent to serving the false gods themselves, neither of which things is befitting to the servants of God" (*Comm.* Ch. 3, v. 18).

St. Jerome notes how the king's anger is totally inordinate; he has been completely overcome by his emotions. So much so that his face was changed with the fury. The fire itself becomes a kind of sign of how great his anger was. He says, "Just as if the usual fire without multiplied intensity could not have consumed the youths' bodies! But a fury and rage which borders on madness can observe no bounds" (*Comm.* Ch. 3, v. 19-20).

Because of the king's anger, the fire is stoked to an outrageous level and it consumes his own servants. St. Jerome says, "Of course this meant the same men of whom it was said above . . . And so they were not any chance servants of his whom Nebuchadnezzar destroyed, but men who of all his army were strong and most ready for war" (*Comm.* Ch. 3, v. 22).

MEDITATIO

1. God is Victorious

There is something very subtle yet crucial here about how we perceive our lives as Christians. In the very midst of their trial, the three young men reclaimed that God was their Savior. They don't conceive of His salvation as hypothetical or distant, but as ontologically foundational truth.

So how do we think of Christ's victory? First of all, do we realize He is King *now*? It is not as if He won the victory and at the end of time He will come back as King. No—He is already victorious, and He already reigns as Lord and King. This is why we can pray to Him and pray with absolute confidence, even when we are in the midst of terrible trials. "For though I should walk in the midst of the shadow of death, I will fear no evils, for thou art with me" (Ps. 22:4a).

So, do we pray to Him as the forever-reigning King of the universe, or do we pray with timidity?

2. What's the Big Deal?

Is it really so bad to offer a little incense or bow down to this golden statue? We know the first commandment is "Thou shall not have other gods besides me." And we might be able to say that if there was a golden statue in front of us we would not worship it. However, there are issues our culture largely considers to be "not a big deal" or "just for fun"—such as idolizing celebrities, dabbling in tarot or astrology, or placing careers and possessions before God—but these issues are serious and demand us to be vigilant.

The Church will always be counter cultural in some way. In our day it is her moral teaching that stands in opposition to the world. There are certain controversies that our culture sees as already settled, such as gay marriage, abortion, and birth control. Such issues have become idol-like, and our current culture almost demands we bow in support of them. But we must seek to speak the truth when called upon. We need the prudence but also the courage of St. Thomas Moore to know when and how. We should not be obnoxious Bible thumpers, but we need to speak the truth courageously when we are called to do so.

3. Emotions

How thin the king is. In the last chapter, he was praising Daniel and his friends, but now he is totally overcome by his own emotions.

It is just as important to know what *not* to do as to know what to do. The king is an example of what not to do. We must not allow ourselves to be swept away by our emotions. There are many adults whose emotional lives are so stunted that they act like children. Two scenarios are a good examination for us: driving and family. When you are in traffic, how quickly does road rage rise up in you? If it's high, that is not normal. That is a result of our fallen nature. When you are with your parents or relatives, how quickly do you start acting like a twelve-year-old and become irritable? That is also not normal.

The rage borders on madness, insanity, and in a certain sense it is. The effect of original sin in our soul is that it darkens the intellect and weakens the will. See that the king's intellect truly is darkened. It is insane because it is not sane to think that a lesser fire will not burn them just as much, will not kill them just the same. His will is subject to his emotions. His soul is totally out of order.

4. Evil Consumes Itself

While anger as an emotion is not a sin in itself, it can lead us into the capital sin of anger if we are not careful. The image of the men being overtaken by the fire they are stoking shows us how evil is always consuming itself. If we let our anger run amuck, it will lead us into the fire of rage, which may hurt others but will definitely hurt us. It will destroy the peace that we are meant to have with Christ. So we should keep a check on our anger and take St. Paul's advice: "Be angry, and sin not. Let not the sun go down upon your anger. Give not place to the devil" (Eph. 4:26–27).

ORATIO

1. How has Christ been victorious in my life? How can I believe He is victorious in a difficult situation in my life right now?

2. Are my emotions out of order? How can I be honest about how I feel? Not letting my emotions run the show, but also not repressing them?

3. Is there someone or some situation that I have deep anger about? Have I asked the Holy Spirit for help?

CONTEMPLATIO

LECTIO: DANIEL 3:24–45

SUBJECT: PRAYING IN COMMUNION, PRAYING IN EXILE, PRAYING WITH CONTRITION.

24 **And they walked in the midst of the flame, praising God
and blessing the Lord.** 25 Then Azarias standing up prayed in
this manner, and opening his mouth in the midst of the fire, he
said: 26 Blessed art thou, O Lord, the God of our fathers, and thy
name is worthy of praise, and glorious for ever: 27 For thou art just
in all that thou hast done to us, and all thy works are true, and thy
ways right, and all thy judgments true. 28 For thou hast executed
true judgments in all the things that thou hast brought upon us,
and upon Jerusalem the holy city of our fathers: for according
to truth and judgment, thou hast brought all these things upon
us for our sins. 29 For we have sinned, and committed iniquity,
departing from thee: and we have trespassed in all things: 30 And
we have not hearkened to thy commandments, nor have we observed nor done as thou hadst commanded us, that it might go
well with us. 31 Wherefore all that thou hast brought upon us,
and every thing that thou hast done to us, thou hast done in true
judgment: 32 And thou hast delivered us into the hands of our
enemies that are unjust, and most wicked, and prevaricators, and
to a king unjust, and most wicked beyond all that are upon the
earth. 33 And now we cannot open our mouths: we are become
a shame and reproach to thy servants, and to them that worship
thee. 34 Deliver us not up for ever, we beseech thee, for thy name's
sake, and abolish not thy covenant. 35 And take not away thy mercy from us for the sake of Abraham thy beloved, and Isaac thy servant, and Israel thy holy one: 36 To whom thou hast spoken, promising that thou wouldst multiply their seed as the stars of heaven,
and as the sand that is on the sea shore. 37 For we, O Lord, are
diminished more than any nation, and are brought low in all the
earth this day for our sins. 38 Neither is there at this time prince,
or leader, or prophet, or holocaust, or sacrifice, or oblation, or
incense, or place of first fruits before thee, 39 That we may find thy
mercy: nevertheless in a contrite heart and humble spirit let us be
accepted. 40 As in holocausts of rams, and bullocks, and as in thousands of fat lambs: so let our sacrifice be made in thy sight this day,
that it may please thee: for there is no confusion to them that trust

in thee. [41] And now we follow thee with all our heart, and we fear thee, and seek thy face. [42] Put us not to confusion, but deal with us according to thy meekness, and according to the multitude of thy mercies. [43] And deliver us according to thy wonderful works, and give glory to thy name, O Lord: [44] And let all them be confounded that shew evils to thy servants, let them be confounded in all thy might, and let their strength be broken. [45] And let them know that thou art the Lord, the only God, and glorious over all the world.

Reading with Saint Jerome

As the three young men are thrown into the fire, they speak praises to God. St. Jerome holds them up as an example for us in our sufferings. He tells us, "Whenever we are oppressed by various anxieties, let us lovingly speak forth this sentiment with our whole heart, and whatever may have befallen us, let us confess that it is only right for us to endure it" (*Comm.* Ch. 3, v. 26).

Although the three young men were not actually guilty, they confessed the sins of the people as if they were their own. St. Jerome says, "Now of course the three youths had not sinned, nor were they old enough when brought to Babylon to warrant being punished for their own faults. Consequently they were speaking as representatives of their people" (*Comm.* Ch. 3, v. 29).

St. Jerome says that this prayer can be used by the Church when she is experiencing different sufferings "because of the sins of the people . . . and also whenever in times of persecution no sacrifice or oblation is offered up" (*Comm.* Ch. 3, v. 37).

St. Jerome likewise explains that this prayer of contrition can be seen in conjunction with David's prayer, "With burnt offerings thou wilt not be delighted. A sacrifice to God is an afflicted spirit: a contrite and humbled heart, O God, thou wilt not despise (Ps. 50:18b–19)" (*Comm.* Ch. 3, v. 39).

MEDITATIO

1. Prayer in Communion

What an example of humble prayer! Our sins have merited us hell, but grace has won us salvation. Whatever punishment and pain we experience, God is completely justified. Think of Job's lament, and how God answers him very clearly. "Who do you think you are? Were you there when I created the universe?" (cf. Job 38:1–7).

And here the young man does not try to distinguish himself from the nation of Israel. He doesn't say, "I have not sinned even though the people have." No, he instead says "we," just as the Lord teaches us to pray "forgive us our trespasses," Do not just forgive me alone, but forgive us. So we should pray with the whole Church, "Forgive us! We have all sinned. We have all had abortions, we have all committed adultery, we have all rejected You because we are one, we are one Church, one Mystical Body of Christ. So please forgive us all!"

2. Prayer in Exile

The young man is praying as an exile. The literal meaning is that the people of God have been brought to Babylon. The temple has been destroyed; there are no sacrifices offered to God; there is no king in Israel; their whole land has been uprooted.

Yet, the Lord was faithful to His people, even in exile. Although their unfaithfulness brought them into desolation, He is still faithful. Although they denied Him in their sins, He cannot deny Himself (1 Timothy). But this shows us that whatever state our unfaithfulness has led us to, if we turn to God now, He will turn to us. If our sins have led us into addiction, then we can turn to Him and pray, "Lord, although I have abandoned You and my sins have led me to the exile of addiction, I beg You to be with me now."

But this should also create a deep gratitude in us for the gift of being able to go to Mass and receive the sacraments. During World War II, there was an entire diocese in Luxembourg whose priests were all arrested and brought to Nazi work camps. That means in one day an entire diocese had no sacraments. Can you imagine? Would we still be faithful if such a thing happened to us?

3. Prayer of Contrition.

Here, the young man prays, as if to say, "Even though there are no sacrifices because the temple is destroyed, then see my contrition as a worthy sacrifice." Here again, we see God's providence. He uses this terrible situation of the exile, brought about by the people's own sins, as the occasion to bring them closer to the real meaning of forgiveness and contrition. The Church teaches that there is such a kind of deep, true contrition that can even wipe away sin. Do we ever confess our sins with such intensity that our heart is crushed like this?

ORATIO

1. Do I see my brothers and sisters as one with me in the Body of Christ, or do I try to keep them separate? Do I pray with a sense of communion, that is, as a "we" not just "me"?

2. Do I appreciate the gifts of the sacraments in my life? Do I receive them regularly? In times of sorrow and exile, do I turn toward God, or only grow angry and despair?

3. Am I truly sorry for my sins? Do I make a full examination of my conscience daily? Do I try to allow God's grace and providence to work in my life, even if I do not understand God's timing?

CONTEMPLATIO

LECTIO: DANIEL 3:46–50

Subject: Vexation of the Heart and Soul, Angelic Help

46 Now the king's servants that had cast them in, ceased not to
heat the furnace with brimstone, and tow, and pitch, and dry
sticks, 47 **And the flame mounted up above the furnace nine**
and forty cubits: 48 And it broke forth, and burnt such of the
Chaldeans as it found near the furnace. 49 But the angel of
the Lord went down with Azarias and his companions into
the furnace: and he drove the flame of the fire out of the fur-
nace, 50 And made the midst of the furnace like the blowing of
a wind bringing dew, and the fire touched them not at all, nor
troubled them, nor did them any harm.

Reading with Saint Jerome

If we take a step back and look at the story thus far, it might seem difficult to understand the purpose of the young men's trials. Yet, continuously, they do not despair; rather, they rise up in faith even stronger each time. And, as always, God never abandons them. St. Jerome sees the trial by fire and the aid of the angel as a great consolation to our spiritual lives and the trials we find ourselves in.

Jerome tells us, "When the soul is oppressed with tribulation and taken up with various vexations, having lost hope of human aid and turned with its whole heart to God, an angel of the Lord descends to it . . . That is to say, the supernatural being descends to the aid of the servant and dashes aside the fierce heat of the violent flames, that the fiery shafts of the enemy utterly fail to pierce the inner citadel of our heart and we escape being shut up in his fiery furnace" (*Comm.* Ch. 3, v. 49).

Again, we see how the Lord ultimately strengthens the young men through trials. God does not Himself create such wickedness as the king's and merely throw us into the fray. Rather, He permits it to happen to these young men as a means of drawing them closer to Him. And out of evil, God creates goodness, He creates something beautiful. Through this, His faithful are brought into a closer union with Him.

MEDITATIO

The literal meaning of this passage tells of how crushed olives could have been used as kindling for the fire and how the angel of the Lord came to the three young men in the fire.

St. Jerome explains that a common opinion is that, "naphtha is the name applied to olive-pits which are thrown away when the dregs of the oil have dried up. In the same way, they assert, the Greek term *pyrine* is derived from its property of nourishing *pyr*, that is, 'fire'" (*Comm.* Ch. 3, v. 46).

But there is a spiritual meaning too, one that points us toward Christ.

1. Crushed hearts

Olives, once crushed, are thrown into the fire, a symbol of crushed hearts. Jesus prayed at the Mount of Olives and this is when His heart was crushed by the sins of the world, when He threw Himself into the fire of God's wrath and love. And just as an angel comes to aid and comfort the three young men, an angel likewise strengthened Jesus in the garden as He was being crushed for our sins (Luke 22:43).

Sometimes we experience the weight of our own sins in a very real way. God can give us a penetrating understanding of what our sins have done to ourselves, to others, and most especially what they have done to Jesus. When we feel this weight, we should throw ourselves into the arms of Jesus, pray with Him in the garden, and console Him with our love and contrition.

2. Angelic help

If we have a sacramental view of reality, we can start to see the real meaning of things. The physical meaning is a sign that points to the spiritual. The angel of the Lord came and saved the men from a literal fire. But this was a sign to show us how God can protect us in fires that are much more dangerous. The literal fire the men escaped was threatening their physical life, but when we suffer the fire of temptation, we are in danger of spiritual death.

Jesus Himself suffered the fire of demonic temptation in the desert, but afterwards the angels came and ministered to Him (Matt. 4:11).

When we experience these kinds of fires, we must draw close to Jesus, because He Himself knows very well what it is like and He can help us overcome our temptations just as He overcame His own. While we might feel afraid or close to despair in such times, we must remember to run from those fires and throw ourselves toward Jesus and His loving embrace.

ORATIO

1. In times of great trial or suffering, do I let myself fall into despair? Or do I run toward God's love and seek His help?

2. Do I regularly pray the Saint Michael prayer for protection? Do I make it a point to pray to my Guardian Angel daily and especially in times of temptation?

3. Do I pray for God's grace and wisdom to show me the way through the "fires" of my life? Do I pray for strength to overcome temptation and tribulation?

CONTEMPLATIO

LECTIO: DANIEL 3:51–90

Subject: Prayer in Tribulation, Humility, Creation Praises God

51 Then these three as with one mouth praised, and glorified, and
blessed God in the furnace, saying: 52 Blessed art thou, O Lord
the God of our fathers: and worthy to be praised, and glorified,
and exalted above all for ever: and blessed is the holy name of
thy glory: and worthy to be praised, and exalted above all in all
ages. 53 Blessed art thou in the holy temple of thy glory: and exceedingly
to be praised, and exceeding glorious for ever. 54 Blessed
art thou on the throne of thy kingdom, and exceedingly to be
praised, and exalted above all for ever. 55 Blessed art thou, that
beholdest the depths, and sittest upon the cherubims: and worthy
to be praised and exalted above all for ever. 56 Blessed art thou in
the firmament of heaven: and worthy of praise, and glorious for
ever. 57 **All ye works of the Lord, bless the Lord: praise and exalt
him above all for ever. 58 O ye angels of the Lord, bless the
Lord: praise and exalt him above all for ever. 59 O ye heavens,
bless the Lord: praise and exalt him above all for ever.** 60 O all
ye waters that are above the heavens, bless the Lord; praise and
exalt him above all for ever. 61 O all ye powers of the Lord, bless
the Lord: praise and exalt him above all for ever. 62 O ye sun and
moon, bless the Lord: praise and exalt him above all for ever. 63 O
ye stars of heaven, bless the Lord: praise and exalt him above all for
ever. 64 O every shower and dew, bless ye the Lord: praise and exalt
him above all for ever. 65 O all ye spirits of God, bless the Lord:
praise and exalt him above all for ever. 66 O ye fire and heat, bless
the Lord: praise and exalt him above all for ever. 67 O ye cold and
heat, bless the Lord: praise and exalt him above all for ever. 68 O ye
dews and hoar frosts, bless the Lord: praise and exalt him above all
for ever. 69 O ye frost and cold, bless the Lord: praise and exalt him
above all for ever. 70 O ye ice and snow, bless the Lord: praise and
exalt him above all for ever. 71 O ye nights and days, bless the Lord:
praise and exalt him above all for ever. 72 O ye light and darkness,
bless the Lord: praise and exalt him above all for ever. 73 O ye
lightnings and clouds, bless the Lord: praise and exalt him above
all for ever. 74 O let the earth bless the Lord: let it praise and exalt
him above all for ever. 75 O ye mountains and hills, bless the Lord:

praise and exalt him above all for ever. 76 O all ye things that spring
up in the earth, bless the Lord: praise and exalt him above all for
ever. 77 O ye fountains, bless the Lord: praise and exalt him above
all for ever. 78 O ye seas and rivers, bless the Lord: praise and exalt
him above all for ever. 79 O ye whales, and all that move in the wa-
ters, bless the Lord: praise and exalt him above all for ever. 80 O all
ye fowls of the air, bless the Lord: praise and exalt him above all for
ever. 81 O all ye beasts and cattle, bless the Lord: praise and exalt
him above all for ever. 82 O ye sons of men, bless the Lord, praise
and exalt him above all for ever. 83 O let Israel bless the Lord: let
them praise and exalt him above all for ever. 84 O ye priests of the
Lord, bless the Lord: praise and exalt him above all for ever. 85 O ye
servants of the Lord, bless the Lord: praise and exalt him above all
for ever. 86 O ye spirits and souls of the just, bless the Lord: praise
and exalt him above all for ever. 87 O ye holy and humble of heart,
bless the Lord: praise and exalt him above all for ever. 88 O Ana-
nias, Azarias, and Misael, bless ye the Lord: praise and exalt him
above all for ever. For he hath delivered us from hell, and saved
us out of the hand of death, and delivered us out of the midst of
the burning flame, and saved us out of the midst of the fire. 89 O
give thanks to the Lord, because he is good: because his mercy
endureth for ever and ever. 90 O all ye religious, bless the Lord the
God of gods: praise him and give him thanks, because his mercy
endureth for ever and ever.

Reading with Saint Jerome

Amid tribulation in the fires and witnessing God's saving mercy, the three young men begin to praise God with a beautiful prayer. This passage, "The Canticle of the Three Young Men," is in fact part of Church's official prayer, the "Liturgy of the Hours." St. Jerome draws us even deeper here, showing how every aspect of creation praises God, not through verbal prayers but by their very being. He writes, "But all creation praises God not in word but in deed, inasmuch as the Creator is logically apprehended on the basis of His creatures, and in the various works and affections . . . the grandeur of God is made manifest" (*Comm.* Ch. 3, v. 57–58).

"O ye holy and humble of heart, bless the Lord: praise and exalt him above all for ever."From this passage Jerome connects humility and poverty in spirit. He says, "We are taught to have humbleness of heart both by this present verse and also by the statement in the Gospel: 'Learn of Me, for I am meek and lowly in heart, and ye shall find rest for your souls' (Matt. 11:29). But this humbleness of heart is the same thing as is elsewhere called poverty in spirit, so that we are not to be lifted up in pride or seek after glory by a pretended humility, but rather that we abase ourselves with our whole heart" (*Comm.* Ch. 3, v. 87).

In this way, when our hearts and deeds are truly humble, we too are able praise God by our very being.

MEDITATIO

1. Learning from Creation

St. Jerome points out that we can learn from creation itself. Think of how humbling this is for us. We can learn from things that do not have rational souls, such as the sun and the wind, how to praise God. Even inanimate objects such as rocks and the moon can teach us how to bless God? How is this possible? Because they bless God by their very nature. There is no sin in them, no rebellion, so just by their very being they sing the praises of God. There are certain saints, like St. Kevin and St. Francis, who perceived God beautifully through His creatures. If we have the sacramental vision they had, we too will see God present in His creation and be brought into imitating creation itself by blessing God. The more truly we can be who God created us to be, the more we will bless God by our existence. This is what St. Irenaeus meant when he said, "The Glory of God is man fully alive." This means man fully infused with divine grace and drawn into the praise of God.

2. Actions Speak Louder Than Words.

There is a second lesson we can learn from creation: actions speak louder than words.

"My little children, let us not love in word, nor in tongue, but in deed, and in truth" (1 John 3:18).

As rational creatures, we are fond of words, but do we bless God by our actions? There is a saying often associated with St. Francis of Assisi, "Preach the Gospel always, and when necessary use words." Francis may or may not have said this, but it is still a powerful counsel for us to remember.

3. Poverty in Spirit

What is humility or poverty in spirit? Humility comes from the Latin, *humus*, meaning ground or earth. This corresponds with Adam being drawn from the soil and the words, "You are dust and to dust you shall return." If we need a trigger for humility, it is the remembrance of our death, *memento mori* (literally, "Remember that you will die").

Monks would often keep a skull on their desk to remind themselves constantly of this fact: someday you will die. Monks put a crucifix on their pillow after waking to remind themselves that someday they will sleep in a casket and a crucifix will be put on top of it. While this might seem rather grotesque, being aware of our mortality, our finiteness, is the basis of humility. We must remember that we are God's creatures, we were drawn from clay, we are dust. Such radical encounter of the possibility of their death brought out humble prayer for the three young men. We too need to engender in ourselves the remembrance of our death and finiteness to foster a deeper spirit of humility.

ORATIO

1. In what ways can I notice God's glory in the world around me? How can my actions or simply my awareness become a form of praise, joining with creation in honoring God?

2. How might my daily actions—my work, my kindness, my integrity—serve as a living prayer, praising God more powerfully and spreading the gospel more than words ever could?

3. How can awareness of my mortality help me live each day more fully for God, cultivating humility and offering my life as a continual praise?

CONTEMPLATIO

LECTIO: DANIEL 3:91–97

Subject: Descent into Hell, Conversion is a Process

91 Then Nabuchodonosor the king was astonished, and rose up in haste, and said to his nobles: Did we not cast three men bound into the midst of the fire? They answered the king, and said: True, O king. 92 **He answered, and said: Behold I see four men loose, and walking in the midst of the fire, and there is no hurt in them, and the form of the fourth is like the Son of God.** 93 Then Nabuchodonosor came to the door of the burning fiery furnace, and said: Sidrach, Misach, and Abdenago, ye servants of the most high God, go ye forth, and come. And immediately Sidrach, Misach, and Abdenago went out from the midst of the fire. 94 And the nobles, and the magistrates, and the judges, and the great men of the king being gathered together, considered these men, that the fire had no power on their bodies, and that not a hair of their head had been singed, nor their garments altered, nor the smell of the fire had passed on them. 95 **Then Nabuchodonosor breaking forth, said: Blessed be the God of them, to wit, of Sidrach, Misach, and Abdenago, who hath sent his angel, and delivered his servants that believed in him: and they changed the king's word, and delivered up their bodies that they might not serve, nor adore any god, except their own God.** 96 **By me therefore this decree is made, that every people, tribe, and tongue, which shall speak blasphemy against the God of Sidrach, Misach, and Abdenago, shall be destroyed, and their houses laid waste: for there is no other God that can save in this manner.** 97 Then the king promoted Sidrach, Misach, and Abdenago, in the province of Babylon.

Reading with Saint Jerome

We should not gloss over the great miracle before us. St. Jerome reminds us, "Let me say again, how wise was the fire and how indescribable the power of God! Their bodies had been bound with chains; those chains were burnt up, whereas the bodies themselves were not burnt" (*Comm.* Ch. 3, v. 92).

There are different interpretations of the nature of the angel who accompanied the young men, but St. Jerome offers his own interpretation: "As for the appearance of the fourth man, which he asserts to be like that of a son of God, either we must take him to be an angel, . . . or indeed, as the majority think, the Lord our Savior" (*Comm.* Ch. 3, v. 92).

The term "son of God" could be used for angels but St. Jerome says in this instance that "this angel or son of God foreshadows our Lord Jesus Christ, who descended into the furnace of hell, in which the souls of both sinners and of the righteous were imprisoned, in order that He might without suffering any scorching by fire or injury to His person deliver those who were held imprisoned by chains of death" (*Comm.* Ch. 3, v. 92).

Beyond this miracle, we again see how God brings forth goodness out of something evil. God used this entire event to elicit the king's faith and conversion once again. St. Jerome says, "A second time, therefore, Nebuchadnezzar resumes a confession of faith in God, and as he condemns idols he praises the three youths who refused to serve or worship any god but their own God" (*Comm.* Ch. 3, v. 95).

For our own spiritual life, we are reminded again that our timing is not God's timing. What we might see as only suffering and tribulation, God sees as an opportunity to share His love and grace evermore.

MEDITATIO

1. Descent into Hell

St. Jerome sees the descent of the angel into the fire as a sign of Christ's descent into hell. Jesus truly descended into hell to bring about His complete victory over sin and death. He robbed the devil of any claim to victory by freeing those waiting in the netherworld.

This descent of Jesus into hell is the absolute victory because He brought love and hope where there was only despair. But this victory now has salvific consequences for us here and now. Not only should it inspire the greatest hope of salvation for us, but it means that when we are in the hell of temptation and suffering, Jesus can come to be with us and free us from any grip of the enemy. Just as He descended into the fire with the three young men, and He descended to hell to bring the fire of His love, so now He descends into our hopeless situations to be our Savior and our comfort.

The chains were burnt, but not their bodies. This is a symbol of purification from attachments. God uses even terrible suffering to bring out a purification in us. St. John of the Cross says that whether it is a string or a chain that is attached to a bird doesn't matter, either way it cannot fly. That is why it needs to be freed. So too for us. And all that is required of us is to cry out, "Deliver us from evil, O Lord!"

2. Conversion is a Process

The king's conversion is a slow series of events. This is the second time he is faced with clear evidence of the one true God. This shows us that conversion is a process.

The word "conversion" comes from the Greek word *metanoia*. The root word *nous* means "mind." To be converted is to have a "change of mind." But not superficially. It means a total and complete change, a transformation of the way we perceive and approach reality. It is a transformation of life: from a life centered on self to a life centered on God. If we see it this way, then we can see that conversion is not a "one and done" kind of thing. It is a life-long process. It was like this for Nebuchadnezzar, and it is no different for us.

We need to learn patience with ourselves in our process of conversion. Sometimes the Lord allows us to struggle with a certain sin for a long time. Obviously He does not desire us to sin, but why would He let us suffer this temptation for so long? Is it to create patience? Is it to make us more humble or more reliant on Him? Yes, and more!

Hopefully it will create in us humility and a real patience for others. We are all in process. We are all pilgrims on the way, so let us not judge one another, but learn patience and kindness wherever we are at on the journey.

ORATIO

1. Have I let Jesus come into the depths of my soul? Do I try to keep Him from the darkest places? Or do in realize this is precisely where I need Him the most?

2. Am I patient with myself? Can I be more patient with others?

CONTEMPLATIO

LECTIO: DANIEL 3:98–4:6

Subject: God or Beasts

98 Nabuchodonosor the king, to all peoples, nations, and tongues, that dwell in all the earth, peace be multiplied unto you. 99 The most high God hath wrought signs and wonders toward me. It hath seemed good to me therefore to publish 100 His signs, because they are great: and his wonders, because they are mighty: and his kingdom is an everlasting kingdom, and his power to all generations.

Chapter 4

1 I, Nabuchodonosor, was at rest in my house, and flourishing in my palace: 2 I saw a dream that affrighted me: and my thoughts in my bed, and the visions of my head troubled me. 3 Then I set forth a decree, that all the wise men of Babylon should be brought in before me, and that they should shew me the interpretation of the dream. 4 Then came in the diviners, the wise men, the Chaldeans, and the soothsayers, and I told the dream before them: but they did not shew me the interpretation thereof: 5 Till their colleague Daniel came in before me, whose name is **Baltasar, according to the name of my god**, who hath in him the spirit of the holy gods: and I told the dream before him. 6 Baltasar, prince of the diviners, because I know that thou hast in thee the spirit of the holy gods, and that no secret is impossible to thee: tell me the visions of my dreams that I have seen, and the interpretation of them.

Reading with Saint Jerome

King Nabuchodonosor wrote this letter and had it published throughout his kingdom in order to recount the dramatic events that happened to him.

St. Jerome explains, "Because he displeased God, Nebuchadnezzar was turned into a madman and dwelt for seven years amongst the brute beasts and was fed upon the roots of herbs" (Comm Ch. 4, v. 1).

But these events brought about a deep conversion in the king and, "Afterwards by the mercy of God he was restored to his throne, and praised and glorified the King of heaven, on the ground that all His works are truth and His ways are justice and He is able to abase those who walk in pride" (Comm Ch 4, v. 1).

MEDITATIO

God or Beasts

In this chapter, we will see the episode of King Nebuchadnezzar becoming beast-like and roaming in the fields for seven years.

This scenario seems fantastic, that an esteemed king could become like an animal, eating grass and living in a field. But have you ever experienced elderly people in a state of severe dementia? Or someone with severe mental and physical handicaps? There are people who suffer from natural phenomena such as these that can act "animalistic." So can we not see that if the Lord sent this as a scourge it is certainly possible?

For Nebuchadnezzar, the choice is to be with God or become an animal. Does this seem strange? It shouldn't. Because this choice has always been ours as well. In Genesis 1, man and woman were created on the sixth day, the same day as the animals. This seems odd. If man and woman are the apex of creation, then why aren't they created on their own separate day? It is because we were created with a choice before us: God or beasts. The sixth day represents earth, but the Sabbath rest of the seventh day represents heaven. We are created on the precipice between earth and heaven, between time and eternity. We are made of earthly stuff, but heaven is our true home. We can choose to stay on the sixth day and live a bestial existence, or we can choose to move to the seventh day and live Divine life.

ORATIO

1. Am I overly concerned with human affairs? Do I value the temporal over the sacred?

2. What am I attached to in this world? What is keeping me from moving toward heavenly life?

CONTEMPLATIO

LECTIO: DANIEL 4:7–15

Subject: Humility, Praying Always

7 **This was the vision of my head in my bed: I saw, and behold a tree in the midst of the earth, and the height thereof was exceeding great.** 8 The tree was great, and strong: and the height thereof reached unto heaven: the sight thereof was even to the ends of all the earth. 9 Its leaves were most beautiful, and its fruit exceeding much: and in it was food for all: under it dwelt cattle, and beasts, and in the branches thereof the fowls of the air had their abode: and all flesh did eat of it. 10 I saw in the vision of my head upon my bed, and behold **a watcher**, and a holy one came down from heaven. 11 He cried aloud, and said thus: Cut down the tree, and chop off the branches thereof: shake off its leaves, and scatter its fruits: let the beasts fly away that are under it, and the birds from its branches. 12 Nevertheless leave the stump of its roots in the earth, and let it be tied with a band of iron, and of brass, among the grass, that is without, and let it be wet with the dew of heaven, and let its portion be with the wild beasts in the grass of the earth. 13 **Let his heart be changed from man's**, and let a beast's heart be given him; and let seven times pass over him. 14 This is the decree by the sentence of the watchers, and the word and demand of the holy ones; **till the living know that the most High ruleth in the kingdom of men**; and he will give it to whomsoever it shall please him, and he will appoint the basest man over it. 15 I king Nabuchodonosor saw this dream: thou, therefore, O Baltasar, tell me quickly the interpretation: for all the wise men of my kingdom are not able to declare the meaning of it to me: but thou art able, because the spirit of the holy gods is in thee.

Reading with Saint Jerome

The greatness of the tree in the vision is a symbol of pride and represents the king himself. But St. Jerome says, "It was not only of Nebuchadnezzar, King of the Chaldeans, but also of all impious men that the prophet says: 'I beheld the impious man highly exalted and lifted up like the cedars of Lebanon' (Ps. 36:35)" (*Comm.* Ch. 4, v. 7).

St. Jerome warns us of the example of those lifted up by pride. This kind of pride will ultimately be cut down in humiliation. He says, "Such men are lifted up, not by the greatness of their virtues, but by their own pride; and for that reason they are cut down and fall into ruin. Therefore it is good to follow the teaching of our Lord in the Gospel: 'Learn of Me, for I am meek and lowly in heart' (Matt. 11:29)" (*Comm.* Ch. 4, v. 7).

St. Jerome says that the word "watchmen," "signifies the angels, because they ever keep watch and are prepared to carry out God's command. And so we too follow the example of the angels in their duties when we engage in frequent night-long vigils" (*Comm.* Ch. 4, v. 10–11).

MEDITATIO

1. Pride Comes Before the Fall

There are many contours of pride that the Book of Daniel displays for us. Here we see the familiar adage "pride comes before the fall." Now St. Jerome points us toward the humble heart of Jesus as the remedy for our pride. Jesus said, "Come to me, all you that labour, and are burdened, and I will refresh you. Take up my yoke upon you, and learn of me, because I am meek, and humble of heart: and you shall find rest to your souls. For my yoke is sweet and my burden light" (Mt. 11:28–30).

The Lord tells us that taking His yoke upon us is the way to find true rest. But what is a yoke, and how do we take His yoke on us? A yoke is a farming tool put on the shoulders of a beast of burden, such as an ox, that enables them to carry heavier weight or drag a plow. At first glance, it seems strange that Jesus would compare Himself to a beast of burden, but it shouldn't. In His divine humility, Jesus did not grasp at glory (cf. Phil. 2), but lowered Himself by becoming man, taking the yoke of the cross on His shoulders, and bearing the full burden of sin for the world. The way of humility is the way of the cross, and it is the only path for us. Jesus invites us to take His yoke on us, that is, to share in His cross. This may mean humiliation, loss of reputation, all kinds of suffering, even death. But if this is the only way to extinguish our pride, then so be it.

2. Watchmen

St. Jerome says the angels are called watchmen because they are always attentive to the Lord. They are always gazing upon Him and attentive to His commands. The question for us is how we can possibly imitate them. St. Jerome notes that Christians of his time perform all night vigils in prayer. But is this even possible? St. Paul says we need to pray always (1 Thes. 5:17). But, in reality, you cannot pray all of the time unless you actually pray *some* time. In Battalia, Portugal, there were monks who prayed the perpetual Rosary for hundreds of years until the French Revolution brought an end to it and cast them out. Almost a hundred years later, Our Lady of Fatima, only a short distance from Battalia, appeared and asked the children to pray the Rosary every day. What if we did the same? Maybe we are not able or perhaps "holy" enough to "pray always," but what if we just started? What if we began with setting aside even a few minutes each day for devout, humble prayer? And what better way than to start by praying the Rosary every day?

ORATIO

1. Where in my life am I still resisting the gentle yoke of Christ, clinging instead to the heavy burden of my own pride?

2. How can I begin, even in a small way, to keep watch with God each day and let prayer become the rhythm of my life?

CONTEMPLATIO

LECTIO: DANIEL 4:16–24

Subject: Can Prayer Change God?

16 Then Daniel, whose name was Baltasar, began silently to
think within himself for about one hour: and his thoughts trou-
bled him. But the king answering, said: Baltasar, let not the dream
and the interpretation thereof trouble thee. Baltasar answered, and
said: My lord, the dream be to them that hate thee, and the in-
terpretation thereof to thy enemies. 17 The tree which thou sawest
which was high and strong, whose height reached to the skies, and
the sight thereof into all the earth: 18 And the branches thereof
were most beautiful, and its fruit exceeding much, and in it was
food for all, under which the beasts of the field dwelt, and the
birds of the air had their abode in its branches. 19 It is thou, O
king, who art grown great and become mighty: for thy greatness
hath grown, and hath reached to heaven, and thy power unto the
ends of the earth. 20 And whereas the king saw a watcher, and a
holy one come down from heaven, and say: Cut down the tree and
destroy it, but leave the stump of the roots thereof in the earth,
and let it be bound with iron and brass among the grass without,
and let it be sprinkled with the dew of heaven, and let his feed-
ing be with the wild beasts, till seven times pass over him. 21 This
is the interpretation of the sentence of the most High, which is
come upon my lord the king. 22 **They shall cast thee out from
among men, and thy dwelling shall be with cattle and with
wild beasts, and thou shalt eat grass as an ox, and shalt be wet
with the dew of heaven: and seven times shall pass over thee,
till thou know that the most High ruleth over the kingdom
of men, and giveth it to whomsoever he will.** 23 But whereas he
commanded, that the stump of the roots thereof, that is, of the
tree, should be left: thy kingdom shall remain to thee after thou
shalt have known that power is from heaven. 24 **Wherefore, O
king, let my counsel be acceptable to thee, and redeem thou
thy sins with alms, and thy iniquities with works of mercy to
the poor: perhaps he will forgive thy offences.**

Reading with Saint Jerome

In this passage, Daniel is asked to interpret yet another of the king's dreams. Here, Daniel makes a striking statement that prompts St. Jerome to ask a fundamental question: since Daniel "had previously pronounced the sentence of God, which of course cannot be altered, how could he exhort the king to deeds of charity and acts of mercy towards the poor?" (*Comm.* Ch. 4, v. 24). In other words, if God had already given His judgement toward the king, why should the king pray for God to change His will?

St. Jerome points to a number of situations in the scriptures where God had already pronounced a harsh judgement before then His will turned to mercy after the repentance of the individuals. Jerome says, "This difficulty is easily solved by reference to the example of King Hezekiah, who Isaiah had said was going to die; and again, to the example of the Ninevites, to whom it was said: 'Yet forty days, and Nineveh shall be destroyed' (Jon. 3). And yet the sentence of God was changed in response to the prayers of Hezekiah and the city of Nineveh, not by any means because of the ineffectualness of the judgment itself but because of the conversion of those who merited pardon" (*Comm.* Ch. 4, v. 24).

St. Jerome shows how it is within God's ability to change His will if we heed His counsel and warnings. "In Jeremiah God states that He threatens evil for the nation (Jer. 23), but if it does that which is good, He will alter His threats to bestow mercy . . . He says that He changes His decision, not with regard to the men themselves, but with regard to their works which have thus changed in character" (Comm Ch. 4, v. 24).

So regarding the king's punishment being delayed, Jerome tells us, "Let us say that Nebuchadnezzar performed deeds of mercy toward the poor in accordance with Daniel's advice, and for that reason the sentence against him was delayed of execution for twelve months" (*Comm.* Ch. 4, v. 24). St. Jerome reminds us that while God's justice is unwavering, His mercy is always near at hand. He is always ready to transform judgment into grace when the sinner repents and turns toward what is good and true.

MEDITATIO

1. Prayer and God's Will

Theologians have long wrestled with questions regarding the relationship between God's sovereign will and man's free will (cf. Boethius, *The Consolation of Philosophy*). Are we really free if God is all powerful? For many of us, this question is not an abstract exercise, but really hits us hard when it comes to prayer. Do our prayers actually mean anything? Can prayers change God? Can our prayers actually effect God's will?

It is mysterious, but it seems that God has worked the possibility of our intercession *into* His own will. He wants us to pray, He wants us to ask, and He wants to intercede. St. Jerome lists a number of examples from scripture where God pronounces a harsh judgement but because of the conversion and prayer of the people, He relents and mitigates His judgement. And He continues to do this today. Our Lady of Fatima told the children that there were certain world events that could be changed depending on our response to God. And if this can happen on the macro, global scale, certainly it can happen in our personal lives too. We should petition God earnestly for the difficult situations in our lives, even if it seems that a decision has already set us in a bad direction.

But even then, why not pray? Think of the Syrophoenician woman (Mt. 15:21–28) who begged Jesus to heal her possessed daughter. At first the Lord ignored her, then He rebuked her, but she continued to ask anyway. The Lord seemed to delight when she relentlessly begged His help, even though He first said no. It is like she said, "I know your will is to deny me, but why not change your will?" We should imitate her creative and persistent way of praying! Why not just ask? For in the mystery of prayer, we discover that God does not change in spite of our petitions, but through them. He changes us, drawing our hearts into the very movement of His mercy and will.

ORATIO

1. What situation in my life seems hopeless? Have I stopped praying about it? How can I pick up prayer again and earnestly beg Jesus for help?

2. Do I truly believe that my prayers can move the heart of God, or have I grown resigned to thinking His will is fixed and distant from me?

3. How might God be inviting me, through persistent prayer, not merely to change my circumstances, but to be changed myself?

CONTEMPLATIO

LECTIO: DANIEL 4:25–34

Subject: Conversion and the purgative way

25 All these things came upon king Nabuchodonosor. 26 At the end of twelve months he was walking in the palace of Babylon. 27 And the king answered, and said: Is not this the great Babylon, which I have built to be the seat of the kingdom, by the strength of my power, and in the glory of my excellence? 28 And while the word was yet in the king's mouth, a voice came down from heaven: To thee, O king Nabuchodonosor, it is said: Thy kingdom shall pass from thee, 29 And they shall cast thee out from among men, and thy dwelling shall be with cattle and wild beasts: thou shalt eat grass like an ox, and seven times shall pass over thee, till thou know that the most High ruleth in the kingdom of men, and giveth it to whomsoever he will. 30 The same hour the word was fulfilled upon Nabuchodonosor, and he was driven away from among men, and did eat grass like an ox, and his body was wet with the dew of heaven: till his hairs grew like the feathers of eagles, and his nails like birds' claws. 31 **Now at the end of the days, I Nabuchodonosor lifted up my eyes to heaven, and my sense was restored to me: and I blessed the most High, and I praised and glorified him that liveth for ever: for his power is an everlasting power, and his kingdom is to all generations.** 32 **And all the inhabitants of the earth are reputed as nothing before him: for he doth according to his will, as well with the powers of heaven, as among the inhabitants of the earth: and there is none that can resist his hand, and say to him: Why hast thou done it?** 33 At the same time my sense returned to me, and I came to the honour and glory of my kingdom: and my shape returned to me: and my nobles, and my magistrates sought for me, and I was restored to my kingdom: and greater majesty was added to me. 34 Therefore I Nabuchodonosor do now praise, and magnify, and glorify the King of heaven: because all his works are true, and his ways judgments, and them that walk in pride he is able to abase.

Reading with Saint Jerome

Although the king's punishment was delayed for a year, he became once again forgetful of God and filled with pride in his own accomplishments. St. Jerome writes, "Because he afterwards while walking about in his palace at Babylon said boastingly: 'Is this not the great Babylon which I myself have built up as a home for the king by the might of my power and the glory of my name?' Therefore he lost the virtue of his charitableness by reason of the wickedness of his pride" (*Comm.* Ch. 4, v. 27).

The king could not rely on his own strength to recover from this fall but was completely dependent on God. St. Jerome explains, "Had he not raised his eyes towards heaven, he would not have regained his former intelligence" (*Comm.* Ch. 4, v. 31).

Some scholars disputed the authenticity of this event, saying that it was mythical and that the king could not have been transformed into a beast. But St. Jerome shows that he became "beast-like," not that he became an actual beast. Jerome argues that when the king "says that his intelligence returned to him, he shows that he had lost not his outward appearance but only his mind" (*Comm.* Ch. 4, v. 31).

This dramatic punishment brought about a dramatic conversion for the king. "Nebuchadnezzar understood the reason why he had suffered in seven years' punishment, and for that reason he humbled himself, since he had exalted himself against God" (*Comm.* Ch. 4, v. 34).

MEDITATIO

1. Occasion of Sin

This situation of the king becoming like an animal is given to us as a sign of what happens to us when we choose sin. But how did he get to this point? Scripture tells us he was "at rest" in his palace. This is reminiscent of when King David walked on his balcony and saw Bathsheba bathing which led to his sins of adultery and murder. What do these kings have in common? The occasion of sin. David had neglected his duty to go to war and became slothful. Nebuchadnezzar was taking rest in his palace, meaning himself. It is when we forget that we are born on a battlefield that we easily fall into sin. We need to remember the words of St. Peter, "Be sober and watch: because your adversary the devil, as a roaring lion, goeth about seeking whom he may devour. Whom resist ye, strong in faith" (1 Pt. 5:8-9).

Too often we find ourselves confused as to how we got into a particular sin. But it is often our neglect to recognize the occasion of sin that leads us to the sin. If we are too much at ease and not aware of the battle, we fall easily. We should take St. Joan of Arc's attitude for our own. During her trial, they tried to trick her and asked her, "Are you in the state of grace?" She said, "If I am, may God keep me there. If I am not, may God put me there."

2. Conversion and the Purgative Way

This extreme situation of King Nebuchadnezzar shows us some of the key aspects of conversion and the beginning of our spiritual life. The first thing we see is that conversion is a *metanoia* which means a "change of mind." When King Nebuchadnezzar "raised his eyes to heaven" his "mind was restored to him." When God sends the grace of conversion to us, our first step is to have a "change of mind." Thus, it is not a flippant decision, but a decision to change the fundamental direction of our life. We need to reexamine how we have lived and be converted from our way to the Lord's way.

But this metanoia is not a "one and done" kind of thing, it is a long process. The king's conversion was long, from the dream about the statue (Dan. 2), to the three young men in the furnace (Dan. 3), all the way through his fall into animalistic existence and his restoration (Dan. 4). All of this was part of his process of conversion. It is no different for us. Before our conversion we lived a vicious life, but our transformation from a vicious to a virtuous life entails a long purification. This first stage of the spiritual life is called the "Purgative way." It is a time when our sinful habits, our worldly attachments, our emotions and every aspect of our soul, need to be purged of selfishness. During this period, we gradually learn to find worldly things distasteful and God's ways sweet. But this can be a painful time of falling in and out of mortal sin until, by grace and perseverance, the Lord brings us through this purgative fire.

ORATIO

1. What are some key moments of grace in my life where I felt God working in my conversion? Did I respond generously?

2. Examine your conscience. What bad habits do you still have that need to be given up? Name one or two habits from the past that need to be purified. Lift them up to God and ask His grace to change.

CONTEMPLATIO

LECTIO: DANIEL 5:1–9

Subject: Practice of the Presence of God, Made for Worship, Circumcision of the Heart

1 Baltasar the king made a great feast for a thousand of his nobles:
and every one drank according to his age. 2 **And being now drunk**
he commanded that they should bring the vessels of gold and
silver which Nabuchodonosor his father had brought away
out of the temple, that was in Jerusalem, that the king and
his nobles, and his wives and his concubines, might drink in
them. 3 Then were the golden and silver vessels brought, which he
had brought away out of the temple that was in Jerusalem: and
the king and his nobles, his wives and his concubines, drank in
them. 4 They drank wine, and praised their gods of gold, and of
silver, of brass, of iron, and of wood, and of stone. 5 **In the same**
hour there appeared fingers, as it were of the hand of a man,
writing over against the candlestick upon the surface of the
wall of the king's palace: and the king beheld the joints of the
hand that wrote. 6 **Then was the king's countenance changed,**
and his thoughts troubled him: and the joints of his loins were
loosed, and his knees struck one against the other. 7 And the
king cried out aloud to bring in the wise men, the Chaldeans,
and the soothsayers. And the king spoke, and said to the wise
men of Babylon: Whosoever shall read this writing, and shall
make known to me the interpretation thereof, shall be clothed
with purple, and shall have a golden chain on his neck, and shall
be the third man in my kingdom. 8 Then came in all the king's
wise men, but they could neither read the writing, nor declare the
interpretation to the king. 9 **Wherewith king Baltasar was much**
troubled, and his countenance was changed: and his nobles
also were troubled.

Reading with Saint Jerome

The question we should ask is why King Baltasar held this banquet and why he would act with such irreverence and contempt toward the vessels brought from the Temple. St. Jerome tells us that the Hebrews had a tradition that God's promise that the Babylonian captivity would last seventy years, as prophesied by Jeremiah and Zechariah, was well known. At the end of that seventieth year, the king wanted to celebrate that this prophecy was false and that the God of the Jews need not be feared. St. Jerome says, "Baltasar had esteemed God's promise to be of none effect; therefore he turned the failure of the promise into an occasion of joy and arranged a great banquet, scoffing somewhat at the expectation of the Jews and at the vessels of the Temple of God. Punishment, however, immediately ensued" (*Comm.* Ch. 5, v. 2).

St. Jerome highlights the danger of excessive alcohol and how this played a part in Baltasar's brazen acts. Jerome says, "This factor also should be borne in mind, that he was not sober when he did these things, but rather when he was intoxicated and forgetful of the punishment which had come upon his progenitor, Nebuchadnezzar" (*Comm.* Ch. 5, v. 2).

St. Jerome notes how absurd it is that they were drinking from golden cups and praising their gods who were made of the same material. Their minds were so blinded that they could not see this irony. "How great was their folly! As they drank from golden vessels, they were praising gods of wood and of stone" (*Comm.* Ch. 5, v. 4).

The fingers writing on the wall of the royal palace had symbolic value. The royal palace was meant to represent the king himself. And the fingers writing on the wall was meant to show the king that God intended to write this message on the heart of the king. St. Jerome says, "The fingers wrote upon the wall of the royal palace in order that the king might understand that the inscription concerned himself" (*Comm.* Ch. 5, v. 5). Baltasar's downfall reveals that when pride and indulgence mock the sacred, God's justice inscribes its warning not on walls alone, but upon the hardened heart that refuses to see.

MEDITATIO

1. Practice of the Presence of God

Because King Baltasar was forgetful of all that happened to his ancestor, Nebuchadnezzar, then he turned to drunken celebration. At first glance, this may seem like there is nothing for us to learn, but there is indeed a key spiritual insight. When we neglect the spiritual, we crave the carnal. Nature abhors a vacuum, and so does supernature. Once we have tasted the sweetness of spiritual things, we need to cultivate a spiritual life that involves daily feeding on the word of the Lord and closeness to God. When we forget about God throughout the day, it is so easy for us to give ourselves over to carnal and unholy things. It can happen so quickly. We think we are doing well in our spiritual lives, and suddenly, we find ourselves back in the throes of sin. Why? We have become forgetful of God's presence. It takes hard work to remain always close to God. The spiritual masters call this the "Practice of the Presence of God." We should get in the habit of recognizing that God is near us; whatever we are doing, He is with us. The saints get to the point where they know this and act throughout the day exactly as they do in adoration or at Mass. They live in perpetual awareness of His closeness to them.

2. Made for Worship

As soon as Baltasar neglects the true God, he begins to praise a false god. This is not accidental but speaks to an absolute truth: We were made for worship. If we don't worship God, we will worship something else. It might be another religion, another person, or even ourselves. But we actually have a need to worship that is written on our hearts.

3. Circumcision of the Heart

There is subtle symbolism in this apparition of the writing on the wall. It is a grace that the Lord had been preparing His people to receive for centuries. The hand of the Lord writes on the royal palace to symbolize writing the message on the heart of the king himself. The exterior message was meant to be internalized by the king. And this is the pattern for us as well. The prophet Jeremiah had previously prophesied a new covenant (cf. Jer. 4:4, 31:33) in which the Lord would write His Law upon our hearts. The new covenant would not be a mere exterior observance of laws written on stone, but an interior embrace of God's Word written on our very hearts. The sign of the old covenant written on stone was circumcision. But the new covenant involves not a mere exterior sign, but the circumcision of our hearts (Deut. 10:16, 30:6). The Lord's heart was pierced on the cross and His blood poured out for us. Our hearts must be pierced too; they must be cut to the core in order for God's grace to really change us from the inside out (Rom. 2:29).

ORATIO

1. When I find myself drifting toward sin, is it because I've forgotten that God is near? How might I begin to live each moment while being more aware of His presence?

2. Do I often examine my affections, imagination, thoughts, and desires? If I am honest, do I worship something other than God? How much time do I spend on the news, sports, or concerned about finances?

3. Have I allowed God's Word to be written on my heart, transforming me from within, or am I still content to follow Him only in outward signs and appearances?

CONTEMPLATIO

LECTIO: DANIEL 5:10–24

Subject: Blindness of Pride, Reward for the Laborer

10 Then the queen, on occasion of what had happened to the king, and his nobles, came into the banquet house: and she spoke and said: **O king, live for ever: let not thy thoughts trouble thee, neither let thy countenance be changed.** 11 **There is a man in thy kingdom that hath the spirit of the holy gods in him: and in the days of thy father knowledge and wisdom were found in him: for king Nabuchodonosor thy father appointed him prince of the wise men, enchanters, Chaldeans, and soothsayers, thy father, I say, O king:** 12 Because a greater spirit, and knowledge, and understanding, and interpretation of dreams, and shewing of secrets, and resolving of difficult things, were found in him, that is, in Daniel: whom the king named Baltasar. Now therefore let Daniel be called for, and he will tell the interpretation. 13 Then Daniel was brought in before the king. And the king spoke, and said to him: Art thou Daniel of the children of the captivity of Juda, whom my father the king brought out of Judea? 14 I have heard of thee, that thou hast the spirit of the gods, and excellent knowledge, and understanding, and wisdom are found in thee. 15 And now the wise men the magicians have come in before me, to read this writing, and shew me the interpretation thereof: and they could not declare to me the meaning of this writing. 16 But I have heard of thee, that thou canst interpret obscure things, and resolve difficult things: now if thou art able to read the writing, and to shew me the interpretation thereof, thou shalt be clothed with purple, and shalt have a chain of gold about thy neck, and shalt be the third prince in my kingdom. 17 **To which Daniel made answer, and said before the king: Thy rewards be to thyself, and the gifts of thy house give to another: but the writing I will read to thee, O king, and shew thee the interpretation thereof.** 18 O king, the most high God gave to Nabuchodonosor thy father a kingdom, and greatness, and glory, and honour. 19 And for the greatness that he gave to him, all people, tribes, and languages trembled, and were afraid of him: whom he would, he slew: and whom he would, he destroyed: and whom he would, he set up: and whom he would, he brought down. 20 But when his heart was lifted up, and his

spirit hardened unto pride, he was put down from the throne of his kingdom, and his glory was taken away. [21] And he was driven out from the sons of men, and his heart was made like the beasts, and his dwelling was with the wild asses, and he did eat grass like an ox, and his body was wet with the dew of heaven: till he knew that the most High ruled in the kingdom of men, and that he will set over it whomsoever it shall please him. [22] **Thou also his son, O Baltasar, hast not humbled thy heart, whereas thou knewest all these things:** [23] But hast lifted thyself up against the Lord of heaven: and the vessels of his house have been brought before thee: and thou, and thy nobles, and thy wives, and thy concubines have drunk wine in them: and thou hast praised the gods of silver, and of gold, and of brass, of iron, and of wood, and of stone, that neither see, nor hear, nor feel: but the God who hath thy breath in his hand, and all thy ways, thou hast not glorified. [24] Wherefore he hath sent the part of the hand which hath written this that is set down.

Reading with Saint Jerome

Daniel had previously been exalted to great leadership in the kingdom under Nebuchadnezzar, but obviously this glory had fallen away so much that Baltasar seemed not even to know him. But St. Jerome notes how Daniel was not attached to these worldly honors, and when promised again with such glory by Baltasar, he shuns it. St. Jerome says, "We should follow the example of a man like Daniel, who despised the honor and gifts of a king, and who without any reward even in that early day followed the Gospel injunction: 'Freely have ye received, freely give'" (*Comm.* Ch. 5, v. 11).

Daniel reminds Baltasar that he already knew the wondrous stories about King Nebuchadnezzar and specifically about his fall into animalism and restoration recounted in chapter 4. He knew about Nebuchadnezzar's conversion and so Baltasar should have known better than to become so filled with arrogant pride against God.

St. Jerome says, "Therefore in thy case also, because thou knewest these things about thy relative and didst understand that God resists the proud and gives grace to the humble, thou shouldest not have lifted up thy heart against the ruler of heaven and scoffed at His majesty and perpetrated the deeds which thou hast" (*Comm.* Ch. 5, v. 22–23).

MEDITATIO

1. The Tension of Christian Ministry

The Christian life involves many tensions, and here St. Jerome highlights the tension of Christian ministry. There are two scriptures that need to be held together in one glance:

"Heal the sick, raise the dead, cleanse the lepers, cast out devils: freely have you received, freely give" (Mt. 10:8) and "The labourer is worthy of his reward" (1 Tim. 5:18b).

What does this mean? Salvation in Christ is a free gift and must not be used in order to make money. This can take many forms such as simony, the selling of blessed objects, certain forms of televangelism, and even religions like Scientology that use money as a barrier to entrance. But these all must be rejected. We received Jesus freely and we must share the gift of Jesus freely.

But that does not mean that professional religious (priests, monks, nuns, etc.) should live in poverty. No, the laborer deserves his payment. We should financially support those who have dedicated themselves completely to the service of the Gospel.

2. You Should Have Known Better

The queen reprimands Baltasar, basically telling him: "You should have known better." The king knew the stories about Nebuchadnezzar and should have remembered how God manifested His glory before, but instead he turned away from the Lord.

But are we any better? If we are honest when it comes to our sins, we too should have known better, we do know better. Even though Jesus makes excuses for us on the cross, "Father, forgive them, for they know not what they do" (Lk 23:34), we should not make excuses for ourselves. We should simply, truthfully, and humbly confess our sins as they are and acknowledge with St. Paul, "For the good which I will, I do not; but the evil which I will not, that I do" (Rom. 7:19). We should simply place ourselves into the infinite mercy of God, even though we do not deserve it.

ORATIO

1. Do I seek recognition and honor in the eyes of the world, or am I content—like Daniel—to serve God freely, trusting that true glory comes only from Him?

2. When I go to confession, do I try to make excuses for myself? Do I try to make my sins sound not so bad, or do I confess them humbly and honestly?

CONTEMPLATIO

LECTIO: DANIEL 5:25–31

Subject: Weighed, Measured, and Found Wanting

25 **And this is the writing that is written: MANE, THECEL,**
PHARES. 26 **And this is the interpretation of the word. MANE:**
God hath numbered thy kingdom, and hath finished it.
27 **THECEL: thou art weighed in the balance, and art found**
wanting. 28 **PHARES: thy kingdom is divided, and is given to**
the Medes and Persians. 29 Then by the king's command Daniel
was clothed with purple, and a chain of gold was put about his
neck: and it was proclaimed of him that he had power as the third
man in the kingdom. 30 The same night Baltasar the Chaldean
king was slain. 31 And Darius the Mede succeeded to the kingdom,
being threescore and two years old.

Reading with Saint Jerome

St. Jerome says that the words written on the wall were simple in definition: "number," "a weighing out," and "removal," but the meaning of these words was not obvious. "And so there was a need not only for reading the inscription but also for interpreting what had been read, in order that it might be understood what these words were announcing" (*Comm.* Ch. 5, v. 25–28).

St. Jerome gives us a clearer exposition to the interpretation. "That God had numbered his kingdom and brought it to an end, and that He had seized hold upon him to weigh him in His judgment-scales, and the sword would slay him before he should meet a natural death; and that his empire would be divided among the Medes and Persians. For Cyrus, the king of the Persians . . . overthrew the Chaldean Empire in alliance with Darius, his maternal uncle" (*Comm.* Ch. 5, v. 25–28).

Needless to say, this message was bad news for Baltasar, so why does he still give Daniel all these gifts? St. Jerome says that this was not strange because the king either "supposed that his predictions would take place in the distant future, or else he hoped he would obtain mercy by honoring the prophet of God. And if he did not obtain this boon, it was because his sacrilege toward God outweighed the honor he accorded to man" (*Comm.* Ch. 5, v. 29).

St. Jerome notes a detail about the historical timing of this banquet. It seems that Babylon had already been at war with

Cyrus and Darius, and now the city had been under siege. So even in this desperate situation he was foolish enough to hold this drunken banquet. "Josephus writes in his tenth book of the *Jewish Antiquities* (Jos. Ant. 10:11) that when Babylon had been laid under siege by the Medes and Persians, that is, by Darius and Cyrus, Baltasar, King of Babylon, fell into such forgetfulness of his own situation as to put on his celebrated banquet and drink from the vessels of the Temple, and even while he was besieged he found leisure for banqueting" (*Comm.* Ch. 5, v. 30–31).

At first glance, it is confusing why Darius becomes king, and then Cyrus afterward. But St. Jerome clarifies, noting, "As for the fact that while Cyrus, King of the Persians, was the victor, and Darius was only King of the Medes, it was Darius who was recorded to have succeeded to the throne of Babylon, this was an arrangement occasioned by factors of age, family relationship, and the territory ruled over. By this I mean that Darius was sixty-two years old, and that, according to what we read, the kingdom of the Medes was more sizable than that of the Persians, and being Cyrus's uncle, he naturally had a prior claim, and ought to have been accounted as successor to the rule of Babylon" (*Comm.* Ch. 5, v. 30–31).

St. Jerome shows that these events were already prophesied by Isaiah (Isa. 13:7) and Jeremiah (Jer. 51:28–33), who declared that God would raise up the Medes to bring judgment upon the proud city (*Comm.* Ch. 5, v. 30–31).

MEDITATIO

1. Weighed in the Scales

Baltasar received a clear judgment of God—he had been weighed on the scales and found wanting. What does it mean to be weighed on the scales, exactly? An image in the ancient pagan work, *The Egyptian Book of the Dead,* explains how the ancient Egyptians believed that after death, the soul had to go on a journey before meeting God in paradise. Along the way, the soul would encounter different trials. One of these trials is called the "weighing of the heart." The soul enters a room where its heart is put on a scale, and on the other side of the scale is just a feather. If the heart weighs more than a feather, then the soul is not worthy to pass on. Yes, this is from a pagan work, but can we gain some insight from it? What does it mean to have a heart as light as a feather? If our hearts are burdened with sin, or burdened with things of the world, then this weighs us down. The good news for us is that this journey to heaven is not something we do on our own. We just need to bring our burdens to Jesus. He said, "Come to me, all you that labour, and are burdened, and I will refresh you" (Matt. 11:28). If we go to him now, we can begin to live heavenly life here.

2. The Radical Mercy of Justice

Why does the king give Daniel gifts after the announcement of his punishment from God? This sounds strange, but is it? There is an unbelievable mercy in meeting the bare justice of God, in meeting reality as it is. Yes, he gives gifts, hoping that his punishment may be mitigated. But he comes face-to-face with reality, and this reality gives him a chance to turn from sin before he dies.

One day when St. Teresa of Avila was at prayer, God showed her in a mystical vision the place that was prepared for her in hell. She saw that the devils had prepared a place like a tiny hole in the wall, filled with darkness and horrible things. A place where she could not sit or lie down or stand up straight. And she tasted for an instant the interior torture of nothing but fire and her soul being torn to pieces. She understood with total clarity that her sins merited her this place, but it was only God's compassion that saved her. She would say later on that this was one of the greatest mercies that God ever gave her.

Do we realize that we have the real possibility of going to hell if we choose? Do we understand that our sins have truly merited us eternal punishment, but God's love is so great that He is constantly saving us from being lost? We should not spend all day thinking about hell, and we should not live in fear of hell. But a little fear of hell goes a long way. If we could just have a little conviction in our souls to remember that we too have the real possibility of going to hell, this tiny little bit of knowledge of reality could spur us onto really pursuing the love of Jesus.

3. In the World but Not of It

This brief historical description of the conquering of the kingdom and its subsequent incarnations is a good reminder that we are called to be in the world but not of it (John 17:14–16). Kingdoms rise and fall, presidents come and go, even popes and bishops live and die, but our faith rests on none of this. Our faith is in Christ Jesus, who is King of the universe. We exist in this world, but we must live for the Kingdom of God.

ORATIO

1. What burdens or attachments are weighing down my heart, and how might I bring them to Jesus so that He can make it light with His mercy?

2. Do I see God's justice as punishment to be feared, or as a merciful invitation to turn from sin and be saved by His love?

3. Where in my life have I allowed the passing kingdoms of this world to distract me from living for the eternal Kingdom of God?

CONTEMPLATIO

LECTIO: DANIEL 6:1–10

Subject: Wisdom, Prayer, and the Upper Room

1 It seemed good to Darius, and he appointed over the kingdom
a hundred and twenty governors to be over his whole kingdom.
2 And three princes over them, of whom Daniel was one: that the
governors might give an account to them, and the king might have
no trouble. 3 **And Daniel excelled all the princes, and gover-
nors: because a greater spirit of God was in him.** 4 And the king
thought to set him over all the kingdom: whereupon the princes,
and the governors sought to find occasion against Daniel with
regard to the king: and they could find no cause, nor suspicion,
because he was faithful, and no fault, nor suspicion was found in
him. 5 Then these men said: We shall not find any occasion against
this Daniel, unless perhaps concerning the law of his God. 6 Then
the princes, and the governors craftily suggested to the king, and
spoke thus unto him: King Darius, live for ever: 7 All the princes
of the kingdom, the magistrates, and governors, the senators, and
judges have consulted together, that an imperial decree, and an
edict be published: That whosoever shall ask any petition of any
god, or man, for thirty days, but of thee, O king, shall be cast into
the den of lions. 8 Now, therefore, O king, confirm the sentence,
and sign the decree: that what is decreed by the Medes and Per-
sians may not be altered, nor any man be allowed to transgress it.
9 So king Darius set forth the decree, and established it. 10 **Now
when Daniel knew this, that is to say, that the law was made,
he went into his house: and opening the windows in his upper
chamber towards Jerusalem, he knelt down three times a day,
and adored, and gave thanks before his God, as he had been
accustomed to do before.**

Reading with Saint Jerome

St. Jerome makes the spiritual meaning of this passage immediately evident. When it says that Daniel went to his "upper chamber" Jerome notes that this is in line with scriptural traditions, along with a prefigurement of the "upper room" that will become so important in the New Testament.

"We must quickly draw from our memory and bring together from all of Holy Scripture all the passages where we have read of *domata,* which mean in Latin either 'walled enclosures' *(menia)* or 'beds' or 'sun-terraces,' and also the references to *anogaia*, that is, 'upper rooms.' For after all, our Lord celebrated the Passover in an upper room (Matt. 14), and in the Acts of the Apostles the Holy Spirit came upon the one hundred and twenty souls of believers while they were in an upper room (Acts 2). And so Daniel in this case, despising the king's commands and reposing his confidence in God, does not offer his prayers in some obscure spot, but in a lofty place" (*Comm.* Ch. 6, v. 10).

In the old covenant, the Temple in Jerusalem was the privileged place of God's presence. The inner sanctuary, the Holy of Holies, housed the Ark of the Covenant where God dwelt with His people. Because of this mysterious presence, all of Judaism was directed toward the Temple in some way.

St. Jerome says that this is why Daniel "opens up his windows towards Jerusalem, from whence he looked for the peace of God" and "also according to what Solomon had said when he admonished the people that they should pray in the direction of the Temple" (*Comm.* Ch. 6, v. 10).

Daniel was in the habit of praying three times a day toward Jerusalem. St. Jerome notes that this practice has been continued in the Church. "There are three times in the day when we should bow our knees unto God, and the tradition of the Church understands them to be the third hour, the sixth hour, and the ninth hour [9:00 a.m., 12:00 p.m., and 3:00 p.m.]" (*Comm.* Ch. 6, v. 10).

St. Jerome tells us that these three hours have taken on new meaning and impetus in the Christian dispensation. For "it was at the third hour that the Holy Spirit descended upon the Apostles (Acts 2). It was at the sixth hour that Peter, purposing to eat, ascended to the upper room for prayer (Acts 10). It was at the ninth hour that Peter and John were on their way to the Temple (Acts 3)" (*Comm.* Ch. 6, v. 10).

MEDITATIO

1. Prayer and the Temple

Even though Jerusalem had been destroyed, Daniel still prayed toward the temple. He opened the window and prayed toward the presence of God. What we have is far greater than what Daniel had. He was only able to pray from a distance toward the former place of God's presence, but we have God truly in our midst. His Eucharistic glory far surpasses what the Jews had in the Ark of the Covenant. But do we have the kind of faith that Daniel had? God dwells with us really and truly in every tabernacle in the world. We need to cultivate a habit of Eucharistic adoration to focus our eyes on the presence of Christ in our midst. Pope St. John Paul II said the spiritual program for the third millennium was to contemplate the Eucharistic face of Christ (NMI, RVM, EDE).

Even if we cannot get to a chapel, we can still make an act of Spiritual Communion and spiritual adoration from where we are. Throughout the day we can pause and adore Him from afar. Then we are really implementing the kind of faith that Daniel had.

2. The Upper Room

The upper room is the locus of the new covenant: in a certain sense the public ministry was just a preparation for the mysteries that would unfold in the upper room. The primary place we encounter Christ is in the sacraments, so think of what was instituted in the upper room. On Holy Thursday, the Lord gave us the priesthood, the men who would communicate the Lord's sacramental life to us. He instituted His new existence in the Eucharist, promising to remain with us always. On Easter Sunday, He gave the apostles the ability to forgive sins in confession. And on Pentecost, the Church received the fulness of the Spirit which we receive in Confirmation. So, are we living Upper Room kinds of lives? Living according to the upper room is to live the resurrected mysteries now. Our entire life must be renewed, it must be a new life in Christ.

3. A Rule of Prayer

The Christian tradition of praying three times a day grew out of the same Jewish custom. As the Church grew and monks lived more intense communal life, three times of prayer became seven times. Diocesan priests today are required to pray five times a day. While different times and places have varied in the way and amount of prayer, they all had a rule of prayer, and this is what we need.

As Christians in the world, we need a rule of prayer maybe even more than monks and nuns. Monks and nuns have the monastery bell that calls them back from work. We need a rule of life that calls us back from the distractions of worldly things to the one thing necessary.

The Benedictine tradition uses the motto *ora et labora*, pray and work. There are too many possibilities for a rule of life and prayer that we cannot describe here, but each of us can start with this simple ideal: pray and work. Create a rule of life that allows you to live the rhythm of prayer and work throughout your day.

ORATIO

1. Do I visit Jesus in the Blessed Sacrament throughout the week? Do I adore Him from afar when I can't? Do I make acts of Spiritual Communion? Am I currently not in the state of grace, or am I in a similar state of life that would prohibit me from receiving Holy Communion?

2. Do I live an "upper room" life? Do I center my daily life on God and His sacraments?

3. What are the key aspects of my daily prayer? Do I have a rule of life? How could I incorporate *ora et labora* into my days?

CONTEMPLATIO

LECTIO: DANIEL 6:11–15

Subject: Dealing with the World

11 **Wherefore those men carefully watching him, found Daniel
praying and making supplication to his God.** 12 And they came
and spoke to the king concerning the edict: O king, hast thou
not decreed, that every man that should make a request to any of
the gods, or men, for thirty days, but to thyself, O king, should
be cast into the den of the lions? And the king answered them,
saying: The word is true according to the decree of the Medes and
Persians, which it is not lawful to violate. 13 Then they answered,
and said before the king: Daniel, who is of the children of the cap-
tivity of Juda, hath not regarded thy law, nor the decree that thou
hast made: but three times a day he maketh his prayer. 14 Now
when the king had heard these words, he was very much grieved,
and in behalf of Daniel he set his heart to deliver him and even till
sunset he laboured to save him. 15 **But those men perceiving the
king's design, said to him: Know thou, O king, that the law of
the Medes and Persians is, that no decree which the king hath
made, may be altered.**

Reading with Saint Jerome

St. Jerome tells us that in observing Daniel's private prayer, "We learn that we are not to expose ourselves rashly to danger, but so far as it lies in our power, we are to avoid the plots of our enemies. And so in Daniel's case, he did not contravene the king's authority in a public square or out in the street, but rather in a private place, in order that he might not neglect the commands of the one true God Almighty" (*Comm.* Ch. 6, v. 11).

St. Jerome tells us that Darius realized that the princes had contrived this whole scenario and, "understood that the princes were making their accusation out of motives of envy" (*Comm.* Ch. 6, v. 15).

But the princes "understood what the king's purpose was, namely that he wished to rescue Daniel from imminent death. And so they allege that according to the law of the Medes and Persians, the commands of a king cannot be nullified" (*Comm.* Ch. 6, v. 15). That is, even King Darius could not undo this law that he himself had made.

MEDITATIO

1. Prudence

St. Jerome's insight not to expose ourselves rashly to persecution leads us to the virtue of prudence. We should be prudent in our dealings with the world. There is a time to make a public stand, but it should not be done imprudently. The Lord even tells us that when they persecute us in one town, we should flee to another (Matt. 10:23).

After Stephen's martyrdom, the Church was scattered from Jerusalem throughout the region (Acts 8:1). When St. Paul was persecuted in one town, he went elsewhere (Acts 14:5). But God uses all of this to serve His mysterious plan. The scattering of the Christians became the means of evangelization. In this way, we are called to "be water." For example, when water flows in a river and comes upon a rock, it does not try to go through the rock, but flows easily around it and still gets where it needs to go. So too when we come up against an obstacle in our life, we should not try to crash through it, but learn to maneuver around it, never "rashly exposing ourselves to danger." Often this is how God is redirecting our path. We are following Him by learning to be water. Not rigid—but learning to sync up with the flow of the Holy Spirit.

2. Uncovering true motives

See how devious these men are. They don't actually care about the king or his decrees. They are seeking to use him for their own evil purposes. We can find two lessons in this: First, "Be ye therefore wise as serpents and simple as doves" (Matt. 10:16b). When dealing with the world we should not be naive. There are in fact people with evil motives, so we need to cultivate shrewdness and not entrust our hearts to every person we meet. But we also need to remember the other part of our Lord's teaching, "Be simple as doves." We need to always purify *our own* motives. We must make sure we are not being deceitful in our own plans, to others or ourselves. In dealing with the world, we are called to offer the humble presence of Christ.

ORATIO

1. When I face obstacles or opposition in living my faith, do I respond with rashness or with the gentle flexibility of "being water," allowing the Holy Spirit to guide my path with prudence?

2. Do I take care to discern the motives of others, and myself, with both the shrewdness of the serpent and the purity of the dove, so that all I do may reflect the sincerity of Christ?

CONTEMPLATIO

LECTIO: DANIEL 6:16–28

Subject: Faith in God, Salvation Through Trial

[16] **Then the king commanded, and they brought Daniel, and
cast him into the den of the lions. And the king said to Dan-
iel: Thy God, whom thou always servest, he will deliver thee.**
[17] And a stone was brought, and laid upon the mouth of the den:
which the king sealed with his own ring, and with the ring of his
nobles, that nothing should be done against Daniel. [18] And the
king went away to his house and laid himself down without taking
supper, and meat was not set before him, and even sleep departed
from him. [19] Then the king rising very early in the morning, went
in haste to the lions' den: [20] And coming near to the den, cried
with a lamentable voice to Daniel, and said to him: Daniel, ser-
vant of the living God, hath thy God, whom thou servest always,
been able, thinkest thou, to deliver thee from the lions? [21] And
Daniel answering the king, said: O king, live for ever: [22] **My God
hath sent his angel, and hath shut up the mouths of the lions,
and they have not hurt me: forasmuch as before him justice
hath been found in me: yea and before thee, O king, I have
done no offence.** [23] Then was the king exceeding glad for him,
and he commanded that Daniel should be taken out of the den:
and Daniel was taken out of the den, and no hurt was found in
him, because he believed in his God. [24] And by the king's com-
mandment, those men were brought that had accused Daniel: and
they were cast into the lions' den, they and their children, and
their wives: and they did not reach the bottom of the den, before
the lions caught them, and broke all their bones in pieces. [25] Then
king Darius wrote to all people, tribes, and languages, dwelling in
the whole earth: PEACE be multiplied unto you. [26] It is decreed
by me, that in all my empire and my kingdom all men dread and
fear the God of Daniel. For he is the living and eternal God for
ever: and his kingdom shall not be destroyed, and his power shall
be for ever. [27] He is the deliverer, and saviour, doing signs and
wonders in heaven, and in earth: who hath delivered Daniel out of
the lions' den. [28] Now Daniel continued unto the reign of Darius,
and the reign of Cyrus the Persian.

Reading with Saint Jerome

We read here how King Darius becomes utterly distraught. He is enmeshed with the world, yet the truth still pierces his conscience. St. Jerome explains that because Darius was unable to stop the plot against Daniel and save his life, "he commits to the power of God the purpose which he himself was unable to attain" (*Comm.* Ch. 6, v. 16).

Darius does not speak with doubt about God's power, "as to say, 'If He be able to deliver thee' but rather he speaks with boldness and confidence and says, 'The God whom thou dost ever serve shall Himself deliver thee'" (*Comm.* Ch. 6, v. 16).

Darius, limited by his own law, does what he can to intercede, even going as far as to seal the rock with his ring, not to keep Daniel in but, "so that the enemies of Daniel might not make any attempt to harm him. For he had entrusted him to the power of God, and although not worried about lions, he was fearful of men" (*Comm.* Ch. 6, v. 17).

St. Jerome says that the fierce nature of the lions was not changed but through divine intervention, "their gaping jaws were closed by the angel, and also their voracious hunger," rather Daniel's faith and good works were before him and seen by God. In this way, his deliverance was not so much a matter of grace as it was a reward for his uprightness (*Comm.* Ch. 6, v. 22).

St. Jerome sees the spiritual meaning of Daniel's deliverance from the lion's den as an allusion for what God does for His chosen ones. For every saint "has been snatched from the mouths of lions unseen and from the infernal pit, because he has trusted in his God" (*Comm.* Ch. 6, v. 22).

MEDITATIO

1. A Rock and a Hard Place

Darius was trapped in an impossible situation. Because of his advisors' scheme, his own authority would now condemn his friend Daniel to death. He was entrapped by his own laws. So, what did he do? He entrusted everything to God. This might sound like an obvious decision, but the truth is we too often forget God and instead rely on ourselves most of the time. We create all sorts of crutches to get through life—friends, alcohol, TV, social media. We don't do it out of malice. In fact, we often don't even realize we are doing it. But the Lord will allow some difficult circumstances to happen in our life in order to make us let go of these crutches. He makes it impossible for us to console ourselves; this is the pivotal moment that leads to total surrender and trust. For many of us, it may not happen until we are faced with death. But what if we started practicing this kind of entrustment now? What if we started depending on Him even before the difficult times come?

2. He Trusted God but not Men

Besides the obvious meaning of sealing the pit to be beyond reproach, St. Jerome sees this act as keeping Daniel safe from the men who plotted against him. Darius comes to the realization that with God, nothing is impossible. At the same time, however, Daniel knows that the evil of men know no bounds. We can almost see Darius weighing the question and answering: "I would rather be in the pit with lions *and* God than with men *without* God." Even in the pit, Daniel is safe because God is with him. This calls to mind Psalm 23 (or Psalm 22 in the Douay-Rheims Bible), "For though I should walk in the midst of the shadow of death, I will fear no evils, for thou art with me."

There is a tradition that Jesus prayed Psalm 129 when He was thrown in the pit while awaiting His trial on Good Friday morning. "Out of the depths I have cried to thee, O Lord: Lord, hear my voice. Let thy ears be attentive to the voice of my supplication . . ." Our Lord has gone before us into the darkness of suffering and death. He has conquered darkness to the point that he owns it. For even darkness is not dark for He is the Light of the world (Cf. Psalm 138:12). In other words, if God is for us, no one can be against us.

3. Angelic Protection

God saved Daniel from lions but He does an even greater work for us. For "the devil, as a roaring lion, goeth about seeking whom he may devour" (1 Pt. 5:8). God not only saved us once and for all on the cross but He still sends angelic protection to guide and guard us even now. We are not alone! God has entrusted us to the care of angels and assigned each of us a guardian angel "to light to guard to rule and to guide." We should cultivate a deep connection and friendship with our guardian angel, talking to him all throughout the day. Our angel has one job: to get us to heaven. And he is completely devoted to this work. It is our job to cooperate with him.

ORATIO

1. When life corners me and my usual comforts fail, do I truly entrust myself to God? Or do I still reach for my crutches instead of His grace?

2. Where in my life am I more afraid of what people can do to me than confident in what God can do for me?

3. Do I live each day with an awareness of my guardian angel's presence and the unseen protection God provides? Do I forget that heaven walks beside me?

CONTEMPLATIO

LECTIO: DANIEL 7:1–12

Subject: Thy Kingdom Come

1 In the first year of Baltasar king of Babylon, Daniel saw a dream:
and the vision of his head was upon his bed: and writing the
dream, he comprehended it in few words: and relating the sum
of it in short, he said: 2 **I saw in my vision by night, and behold
the four winds of the heaven strove upon the great sea.** 3 **And
four great beasts, different one from another, came up out of
the sea.** 4 **The first was like a lioness, and had the wings of an
eagle: I beheld till her wings were plucked off, and she was
lifted up from the earth, and stood upon her feet as a man, and
the heart of a man was given to her.** 5 And behold another beast
like a bear stood up on one side: and there were three rows in the
mouth thereof, and in the teeth thereof, and thus they said to it:
Arise, devour much flesh. 6 After this I beheld, and lo, another like
a leopard, and it had upon it four wings as of a fowl, and the beast
had four heads, and power was given to it. 7 **After this I beheld in
the vision of the night, and lo, a fourth beast, terrible and won-
derful, and exceeding strong, it had great iron teeth, eating and
breaking in pieces, and treading down the rest with its feet:
and it was unlike to the other beasts which I had seen before
it, and had ten horns.** 8 **I considered the horns, and behold an-
other little horn sprung out of the midst of them: and three of
the first horns were plucked up at the presence thereof: and be-
hold eyes like the eyes of a man were in this horn, and a mouth
speaking great things.** 9 **I beheld till thrones were placed, and
the Ancient of days sat: his garment was white as snow, and the
hair of his head like clean wool: his throne like flames of fire:
the wheels of it like a burning fire.** 10 A swift stream of fire issued
forth from before him: thousands of thousands ministered to him,
and ten thousand times a hundred thousand stood before him: the
judgment sat, and the books were opened. 11 I beheld because of
the voice of the great words which that horn spoke: and I saw that
the beast was slain, and the body thereof was destroyed, and given
to the fire to be burnt: 12 And that the power of the other beasts
was taken away: and that times of life were appointed them for a
time, and a time.

Reading with Saint Jerome

Daniel's dream in the opening verses of Chapter 7 present a vision of four beasts rising from the sea, an image that St. Jerome's believes unveils the mystery of earthly kingdoms and the eternal sovereignty of God. Jerome first notes that this vision is anachronistic, revealed "in the first year of Baltasar" but placed here for theological, not historical, reasons. Daniel sees beyond time into the spiritual structure of history. "The four winds of heaven," which Jerome identifies as angelic powers, stir up "the great sea," symbolizing "this world and the present age, overwhelmed with salty and bitter waves" (*Comm.* Ch. 7, v. 2–3).

Four beasts arise from this troubled sea. These are symbols of empires marked by wickedness and pride. The lioness with eagle's wings represents Babylon, royal and exalted, yet brought low. Its torn wings signify the loss of power, and when it stands "like a man" and receives "a human heart," Jerome sees Nebuchadnezzar's conversion, a tyrant restored to reason and humility (*Comm.* Ch. 7, v. 4). The bear is Medo-Persia, fierce yet ascetic; its "three rows of teeth" devour the Babylonian, Median, and Persian realms united under one empire (*Comm.* Ch. 7, v. 5). The leopard, swift and many-headed, signifies Alexander's Greece, whose four heads correspond to his divided successors. "Power was given to it," Jerome writes, "showing the empire came not from valor but from the will of God" (*Comm.* Ch. 7, v. 6). The nameless fourth beast, "dreadful and terrible," is Rome; iron-strong, partaking "of all the more ferocious characteristics we might think of in connection with beasts" (*Comm.* Ch. 7, v. 7).

But above these earthly kingdoms appears the "Ancient of Days," enthroned in fire. "His throne consists of fiery flames," Jerome writes, recalling that "God is a consuming fire" (Deut. 4:24). The books are opened, revealing every conscience before divine judgment, and "the beast was slain," signifying the final overthrow of worldly powers and the blasphemy of the Antichrist (*Comm.* Ch. 7, v. 9–11). Thus, Jerome tell us, "the saints shall never possess an earthly kingdom, but only a heavenly one" (*Comm.* Ch. 7, v. 18). Daniel's prophetic dream tells us that history doesn't culminate in an earthly empire, but in the everlasting reign of God.

MEDITATIO

1. Drinking the Salty Water

St. Jerome says the ocean represents the world and that this water is bitter and salty. That is because the world is filled with waters that do not give us life, but make our thirst greater. If you drink salt water, your thirst becomes worse. The more we seek to find fulfillment in the goods of this world, the worse our hunger becomes. We are never satisfied with this world. St. Augustine said, "Our hearts are restless until they rest in you" (*Confessions 1,1*). If we try to satiate ourselves from this world's goods, we leave with a more terrible thirst.

2. Thy Kingdom Come, Thy Will Be Done

At first glance, it seems difficult to draw out any spiritual meaning from these strange images that Daniel gives us: beasts, feathers, horns, etc. . . . But we do not need to get lost in the details. There is something more fundamental for us to understand. That is, we have a foundational choice in our life: Do I want my own kingdom, or God's kingdom? We see that all earthly kingdoms fall, but God's kingdom is eternal. But how do we choose to live for God's kingdom? The Lord taught us to pray, "Thy kingdom come, Thy will be done." This is the crux of the matter. Of course we want God's kingdom to break through into the world. But it can only come into the world if it first comes into us. We need to make our hearts a throne for Christ to reign in us. We need to enthrone Him as He justly deserves. The King of love deserves to reign in our hearts. But He must not be a dummy-king, a mere figure head. That is why we follow with "Thy will be done."

From one perspective, our entire conversion consists in aligning our will with God's. From the beginning of our fall in the garden, we tried to control our fate, we tried to create our own rules for living by grasping at the tree. In our fallen human nature, we continue to tend toward the rebellious posture of grasping. Now we need to open our hands to receive, not grasp. Conversion involves the transformation of our hands from a posture of grasping to one of receiving. From control to open-handed trust. This is why we need to pray over and over again, "Thy kingdom come, Thy will be done, on earth as it is in heaven."

ORATIO

1. Where in my life am I trying to quench my spiritual thirst with "salty water"? Why do I seek things that promise satisfaction but leave me emptier? How might I turn instead to the living water that Christ offers?

2. Am I living like I am in the kingdom of God? In what areas of my life am I still trying to build my own kingdom rather than letting Christ reign?

CONTEMPLATIO

LECTIO: DANIEL 7:13–28

Subject: The Power and the Glory

13 I beheld therefore in the vision of the night, and lo, one like the
son of man came with the clouds of heaven, and he came even to
the Ancient of days: and they presented him before him. 14 **And
he gave him power, and glory, and a kingdom: and all peoples,
tribes and tongues shall serve him: his power is an everlast-
ing power that shall not be taken away: and his kingdom that
shall not be destroyed.** 15 My spirit trembled, I Daniel was af-
frighted at these things, and the visions of my head troubled me.
16 I went near to one of them that stood by, and asked the truth of
him concerning all these things, and he told me the interpretation
of the words, and instructed me: 17 These four great beasts are four
kingdoms, which shall arise out of the earth. 18 But the saints of
the most high God shall take the kingdom: and they shall possess
the kingdom for ever and ever. 19 After this I would diligently
learn concerning the fourth beast, which was very different from
all, and exceeding terrible: his teeth and claws were of iron: he
devoured and broke in pieces, and the rest he stamped upon with
his feet: 20 And concerning the ten horns that he had on his head:
and concerning the other that came up, before which three horns
fell: and of that horn that had eyes, and a mouth speaking great
things, and was greater than the rest. 21 I beheld, and lo, that horn
made war against the saints, and prevailed over them, 22 Till the
Ancient of days came and gave judgment to the saints of the most
High, and the time came, and the saints obtained the kingdom.
23 And thus he said: The fourth beast shall be the fourth kingdom
upon earth, which shall be greater than all the kingdoms, and
shall devour the whole earth, and shall tread it down, and break
it in pieces. 24 And the ten horns of the same kingdom, shall be
ten kings: and another shall rise up after them, and he shall be
mightier than the former, and he shall bring down three kings.
25 **And he shall speak words against the High One, and shall
crush the saints of the most High: and he shall think him-
self able to change times and laws, and they shall be delivered
into his hand until a time, and times, and half a time.** 26 **And
judgment shall sit, that his power may be taken away, and be
broken in pieces, and perish even to the end.** 27 **And that the**

kingdom, and power, and the greatness of the kingdom, under the whole heaven, may be given to the people of the saints of the most High: whose kingdom is an everlasting kingdom, and all kings shall serve him, and shall obey him. 28 Hitherto is the end of the word. I Daniel was much troubled with my thoughts, and my countenance was changed in me: but I kept the word in my heart.

Reading with Saint Jerome

Daniel's dream continues and the prophet beholds "one like the Son of man coming with the clouds of heaven" (Dan. 7:13) who approaches the Ancient of Days and receives "power, and glory, and a kingdom." St. Jerome interprets this through the light of Christ and declares that "the Son of man . . . is the same as He who, according to John, is called the Lion of the tribe of Judah, the Root of David" (*Comm.* Ch. 7, v. 13). This vision prefigures and tells of the Incarnation and the eternal kingship of Christ. Jerome connects this "Son of Man" to the rock "cut without hands" from Nebuchadnezzar's dream (Dan 2), signifying that Christ "took upon Himself human flesh," the divine Word becoming man to shatter the kingdoms of this world (*Comm.* Ch. 7, v. 13–14).

Jerome further links Daniel's vision to the Transfiguration: "The Savior also, when He was transfigured on the mount and assumed the glory of His divine majesty, appeared in shining white garments" (*Comm.* Ch. 7, v. 14). The radiant Son who reigns eternally is the same who humbled Himself, fulfilling St. Paul's words: "He emptied Himself, taking the form of a servant . . . becoming obedient unto death, even to the death of the cross" (Phil. 2:6–8). The exaltation Daniel foresaw is thus the divine response to the humility of the cross.

But before this final triumph, Jerome warns of the "little horn"—the Antichrist—who "will wage war against the saints" and "exalt himself . . . to attempt changing the very laws of God." Possessed by Satan, he will "sit in the temple of God, making himself out to be like God" (*Comm.* Ch. 7, v. 8, 25). Yet, Jerome assures his reign will not last: "The Antichrist . . . will have his kingdom permanently destroyed" (*Comm.* Ch. 7, v. 26). In this light, Daniel's vision ends in hope; though earthly powers rage, the Son of Man reigns forever, and "the kingdom, and power, and greatness" shall belong to the saints in union with their eternal King.

MEDITATIO

Son of Man

Daniel sees the Son of Man bestowed with divine glory before the throne of God. How are we to understand this mysterious figure of the Son of Man? And what does it mean for us? "Son of man" is a pregnant phrase meaning both humility, as in Psalm 8:5 "What is man that thou art mindful of him? or the son of man that thou visitest him?", as well as divine glory as in the scene before us. And its meaning becomes even more mysterious when Jesus claims this identity for Himself (Mt. 16:13). In fact, Jesus calls Himself the Son of Man eighty-one times in the gospels. But when He does this, is He referring to humility and mere humanity, or apocalyptic glory? It's both.

How are we to hold these two apparent opposites together? The Lord Himself gives us the key: it is nothing other than the cross. When He is asked during His trial if He is the Messiah, He boldly claims, "I say to you, hereafter you shall see the Son of man sitting on the right hand of the power of God, and coming in the clouds of heaven" (Mt. 26:64). Jesus proclaims that His glory as the Son of man is achieved through His passion on the cross. Here is where the glory He had with the Father will be fully on display. If we want to behold the glory of the Son of Man, we must behold the wood of the cross.

But Daniel's vision also gives us a small glimpse into God's eternal plan for humanity, because the plan of His saving Incarnation included us from the beginning. He did not become man for Himself but for us. The *Catechism of the Catholic Church* says:

> "The Word became flesh to make us '*partakers of the divine nature*': 'For this is why the Word became man, and the Son of God became the Son of man: so that man, by entering into communion with the Word and thus receiving divine sonship, might become a son of God.' 'For the Son of God became man so that we might become God.' 'The only-begotten Son of God, wanting to make us sharers in his divinity, assumed our nature, so that he, made man, might make men gods'" (*CCC* 460).

Do we realize how great our dignity is? Do we have a clue how much we are loved by God? The Son of God became the Son of man to make the sons of men into the sons of God. He holds nothing back from us. He wants us to share in His glory. And how do we begin to share His life? It is none other than the Eucharist where we start to experience this transformation. The hymn "O Sacrum Convivium" says it this way:

"O sacred banquet, in which Christ is received, the memory of His Passion is renewed, the mind is filled with grace, and a pledge of future glory given to us."

We need to renew our devotion to receiving Jesus in the Eucharist, because it is in our union with Him that we begin to experience heavenly glory.

ORATIO

1. How can I learn to see the glory of Christ not only in His heavenly majesty but also in His humility, especially in the mystery of the Cross?

2. Do I truly believe that I am called to share in God's own life and glory? How does this truth shape the way I live, pray, and see others?

3. When I approach the Eucharist, do I recognize it as a foretaste of heaven and a participation in the Son of Man's glory? How might I renew my devotion to receiving Him with deeper awe and love?

CONTEMPLATIO

LECTIO: DANIEL 8:1–12

SUBJECT: WINDOW OR MIRROR, THE MAIN THING, BEING A PROPHET

**1 In the third year of the reign of king Baltasar, a vision appeared
to me. I Daniel, after what I had seen in the beginning, 2 Saw
in my vision when I was in the castle of Susa, which is in the
province of Elam: and I saw in the vision that I was over the
gate of Ulai. 3 And I lifted up my eyes, and saw: and behold a
ram stood before the water, having two high horns, and one
higher than the other, and growing up. 4 Afterward I saw the
ram pushing with his horns against the west, and against the
north, and against the south: and no beasts could withstand
him, nor be delivered out of his hand: and he did according to
his own will, and became great.** 5 And I understood: and behold
a he goat came from the west on the face of the whole earth, and
he touched not the ground, and the he goat had a notable horn
between his eyes. 6 And he went up to the ram that had the horns,
which I had seen standing before the gate, and he ran towards
him in the force of his strength. 7 And when he was come near the
ram, he was enraged against him, and struck the ram: and broke
his two horns, and the ram could not withstand him: and when
he had cast him down on the ground, he stamped upon him, and
none could deliver the ram out of his hand. 8 And the he goat
became exceeding great: and when he was grown, the great horn
was broken, and there came up four horns under it towards the
four winds of heaven. 9 And out of one of them came forth a little
horn: and it became great against the south, and against the east,
and against the strength. 10 And it was magnified even unto the
strength of heaven: and it threw down of the strength, and of the
stars, and trod upon them. 11 And it was magnified even to the
prince of the strength: and it took away from him the continual
sacrifice, and cast down the place of his sanctuary. **12 And strength
was given him against the continual sacrifice, because of sins:
and truth shall be cast down on the ground, and he shall do
and shall prosper.**

Reading with Saint Jerome

In Daniel's next vision, St. Jerome helps us locate the time and place. As in the previous chapter, it is not in chronological order of the earlier portion of the book, but the vision in chapter 8, "Came two years after the previous revelation" which "was beheld in the first year of Baltasar, whereas this was beheld in the third year" (*Comm.* Ch. 8, v. 1). St. Jerome tells us that Susa "is the chief city of the region of the Elamites, and there, according to Josephus' account, Daniel erected a lofty tower . . . of such outstanding beauty that it seems newly built even up to the present day. There also the remains of the kings of the Persians and Medes lie buried" (*Comm.* Ch. 8, v. 2).

St. Jerome identifies the ram as "Darius, Cyrus's uncle . . . He reigned over the Medes after his father, Astyages. And the one horn which was higher than the other, and growing still larger, signified Cyrus himself . . . and reigned over the Medes and Persians along with his uncle, Darius" (*Comm.* Ch. 8, v. 3).

The ram in verse 4 is not a personal reference to Darius or Cyrus but refers rather to "the ram of the same kingdom as theirs." For it was "the second Darius, who was the last king of the Persian power . . . who was overcome by the king of the Macedonians, Alexander the son of Philip" (*Comm.* Ch. 8, v. 4).

St. Jerome explains, "Let us simply repeat the words of Gabriel as he explained the prophet's vision. He said, 'The ram whom thou sawest to possess two horns is the king of the Medes and Persians.' This was, of course [the later] Darius the son of Arsames, in whose reign the kingdom of the Medes and Persians was destroyed" (*Comm.* Ch. 8, v. 5).

The he-goat that appeared to not touch the ground "because of his extraordinary speed" was Alexander, the king of the Greeks, who after the overthrow of Thebes took up arms against the Persians and "conquered the generals of Darius and finally smashed against the ram himself and broke in pieces his two horns, the Medes and the Persians. Casting him beneath his feet, he subjected both horns to his own authority" (*Comm.* Ch. 8, v. 5).

The large horn refers to Alexander himself. But when he died, the four horns to replace him would be "his four generals" who "divided his empire among themselves. For Ptolemy, the son of Lagos, seized Egypt; the Philip who was also called Aridaeus, the half-brother of Alexander took over Macedonia; Seleucus Nicanor took over Syria, Babylonia, and all the kingdoms of the East; and Antigonus ruled over Asia Minor" (*Comm.* Ch. 8, v. 5).

The little horn in verse 9 would be Antiochus Epiphanes (who died c. 164 BC) and who "fought with Ptolemy Philometor, that is, 'against the South' and against Egypt; and then again 'against the East' and against those who were fomenting revolution in Persia. At the last he fought against the Jews and captured Judea, entering into Jerusalem and setting up in the Temple of God the statue of Jupiter Olympius" (*Comm.* Ch. 8, v. 9).

St. Jerome explains that when the little horn rose against the "strength of heaven" it means "against the children of Israel, who were protected by the assistance of angels. He pushed his arrogance to such an extreme that he subjected the majority of the saints to the worship of idols" (*Comm.* Ch. 8, v. 9).

When Antiochus glorified himself against the "prince of strength, this means that he lifted himself up against God and persecuted His saints" (*Comm.* Ch. 8, v. 11–12).

Jerome notes that "He even took away the continual offering which was customarily sacrificed in the morning" and the evening, "and he prevailed to the casting down of the 'place of His sanctuary'" (*Comm.* Ch. 8, v. 11–12). But Jerome reminds us that Antiochus "did not do this by his own prowess, but only 'on account of the sins of the people'" (*Comm.* Ch. 8, v. 11–12). Because of the sins of the people "the worship of idols flourished" and "the religion of God suffered an eclipse" (*Comm.* Ch. 8, v. 11–12).

MEDITATIO

1. Window or Mirror

In this chapter, we read the same prophecy given in chapters two and seven regarding the kingdoms that will follow the Babylonian empire. In chapter two, we have the vision of the statue that prophesies four successive kingdoms: Babylon, Medo-Persian, Greek, and Roman. Here in chapter eight, we have only the Medo-Persian, which will conquer Babylon and the Greek kingdom, culminating with Antiochus.

We can look at this prophecy as a window, or as a mirror. Looking through the window gives us a historical perspective. But when we look at it as a mirror, we must contemplate it in a reflective way: what does this vision mean for me, now? When we think of it as a window, we see that it accurately prophesies the history of the successive kingdoms from Babylon through to the Greek conquest of Jerusalem. In a brief historical interpretation, the ram with the two horns is the Medo-Persian empire. The two horns represent Darius and Cyrus. This ram, the Medo-Persian empire, will conquer Babylon as we have seen. The horn that is growing is Cyrus who will succeed Darius. The he-goat that will conquer the ram is the Greek empire, and the singular horn is none other than Alexander the Great. Alexander will conquer so quickly that he will appear to not even touch the earth, but rather will appear to fly across the world. But Alexander died young after conquering the world and was succeeded by four horns; that is, four men who divided up his kingdom. After a while, the little horn that grew is Antiochus, who brought great harm to Jerusalem during the time of the Maccabees. This is where the prophecy ends.

This history is helpful because it gives us confidence in God's revelation. But we need also to look at this prophecy as in a mirror: What does it say to me personally? What is there in this obscure, ancient prophecy that can give me guidance in my spiritual life?

2. The Main Thing

First, an important fact is that God communicated this prophecy to Daniel three times with three different images. This shows that it was an important message from God, and it was clearly a very important part of Daniel's mission to communicate this prophecy to God's people. Much like the saying, "the main thing is to keep the main thing the main thing," this prophecy was definitely the "main thing" for Daniel. But what about us? Sometimes the Lord has an important message for us. We should ask the Holy Spirit what is the main thing we need to hear from Him? What is He trying to tell us?

The Lord will probably not give us dramatic prophetic visions as He gave to Daniel, but He still has very important truths to communicate to us. We may not get direct revelations, but the Lord will give us inspirations, nudges from different directions. Here is one way this could happen: I have a vague sense in my soul that I should go to daily Mass more often. A week later someone tells me how important daily Mass has become in their life. Then someone else sends me an article talking about the effectiveness of receiving frequent Communion. This is probably the Lord nudging me toward daily Mass. He sends the same message in different ways.

3. Being a Prophet

Another meaning we can draw for ourselves from this vision is the call to be a prophet (see *The Catechism of the Catholic Church* 785, 905, 942).

Yes, Daniel had a unique and rare gift of prophecy, but there is a much more ordinary role in being a prophet. At Baptism we are anointed priest, prophet, and king. We are given the vocation to be a prophet. This does not mean prophesying future events through extraordinary revelations: A prophet is the "mouth-piece" or "spokesman" for God. We are prophets when by our words and deeds we bear witness to the Gospel, when we live differently than the world. So are we living this prophetic call? Do we live prophetically? Do we live in a manner that reveals we have been changed by Christ? Can others tell by our lifestyle that we believe in Jesus? Evangelization is not an option; it is a mandate from the Lord to go out into the whole world and share the good news (Mk. 16:15). Do we share the Gospel with others?

ORATIO

1. What might the Lord be trying to tell me? Do I listen?

2. What is the "main thing" in my life? Am I focused on what God is calling me toward?

3. Do I live my life as a prophet for Christ? To I live in a manner that announces the Gospel?

CONTEMPLATIO

LECTIO: DANIEL 8:13–27

Subject: Window or Mirror (continued), False Worship in the Temple

13 And I heard one of the saints speaking, and one saint said to another, I know not to whom that was speaking: How long shall be the vision, concerning the continual sacrifice, and the sin of the desolation that is made: and the sanctuary, and the strength be trodden under foot? **14 And he said to him: Unto evening and morning two thousand three hundred days: and the sanctuary shall be cleansed. 15 And it came to pass when I Daniel saw the vision, and sought the meaning, that behold there stood before me as it were the appearance of a man.** 16 And I heard the voice of a man between Ulai: and he called, and said: Gabriel, make this man to understand the vision. 17 And he came and stood near where I stood: and when he was come, I fell on my face trembling, and he said to me: Understand, O son of man, for in the time of the end the vision shall be fulfilled. 18 And when he spoke to me I fell flat on the ground: and he touched me, and set me upright, 19 And he said to me: I will shew thee what things are to come to pass in the end of the malediction: for the time hath its end. 20 The ram, which thou sawest with horns, is the king of the Medes and Persians. 21 And the he goat, is the king of the Greeks, and the great horn that was between his eyes, the same is the first king. 22 But whereas when that was broken, there arose up four for it: four kings shall rise up of his nation, but not with his strength. 23 And after their reign, when iniquities shall be grown up, there shall arise a king of a shameless face, and understanding dark sentences. 24 And his power shall be strengthened, but not by his own force: and he shall lay all things waste, and shall prosper, and do more than can be believed. And he shall destroy the mighty, and the people of the saints, 25 According to his will, and craft shall be successful in his hand: and his heart shall be puffed up, and in the abundance of all things he shall kill many: and he shall rise up against the prince of princes, and shall be broken without hand. 26 And the vision of the evening and the morning, which was told, is true: thou therefore seal up the vision, because it shall come to pass after many days. 27 And I Daniel languished, and was sick for some days: and when I was risen up, I did the

king's business, and I was astonished at the vision, and there was none that could interpret it.

Reading with Saint Jerome

St. Jerome explains the important note that when the text says "saint" the author is referring to one of the angels (*Comm.* Ch. 8, v. 13). St. Jerome saysthat in verse 13, "One angel asks another angel for how long a period the Temple is by the judgment of God to be desolated under the rule of Antiochus, King of Syria, and how long the image of Jupiter is to stand in God's Temple" (*Comm.* Ch. 8, v. 13).

St. Jerome says that "If we read the Books of Maccabees and the history of Josephus, we shall find it there recorded that . . . Antiochus entered Jerusalem, and after wreaking a general devastation he returned again in the third year and set up the statue of Jupiter in the Temple. Up until the time of Judas Macca-baeus . . . Jerusalem lay waste over a period of six years, and for three [of those] years the Temple lay defiled; making up a total of two thousand three hundred days plus three months (see footnote for full commentary)" (*Comm.* Ch. 8, v. 14).[1]

---

[1] V.14 "If we read the Books of Maccabees and the history of Josephus, we shall find it there recorded that in the one hundred and forty-third year after the Seleucus who first reigned in Syria after the decease of Alexander, Antiochus entered Jerusalem, and after wreaking a general devastation he returned again in the third year and set up the statue of Jupiter in the Temple. Up until the time of Judas Macca-baeus, that is, up until the one hundred and eighth year, Jerusalem lay waste over a period of six years, and for three [of those] years the Temple lay defiled; making up a total of two thousand three hundred days plus three months. [At least that is what the text seems to say, following the present word-order. Actually, the three months should be added to the six years in order to come out to a total of approximately 2300 days.] At the end of the period the Temple was purged. Some authorities read two hundred instead of two thousand three hundred, in order to avoid the apparent excess involved in six years and three months. [Actually, however, 2200 days would come out to only six years and nine days; the reasoning here is unclear.] Most of our commentators refer this passage to the Antichrist, and hold that that which occurred under Antiochus was only by way of a type which shall be fulfilled under Antichrist. And as for the statement, 'The sanctuary shall be cleansed,' this refers to the time of Judas Maccabaeus, who came from the village of Modin, and who being aided by the efforts of his brothers and relatives and many of the Jewish people [defeated] the generals of Antiochus not far above Emmaus (which is now called Nicopolis). And hearing of this, Antiochus, who had risen up against the Prince of princes, that is, against the Lord

In verse 15 Daniel saw someone who had the "appearance of a man" but Jerome teaches us that, "Angels, after all, are not actually men by nature, but they resemble men in appearance. For example, three persons appeared as men to Abraham at the oak of Mamre (Gen. 18), and yet they certainly were not men, for one of them was worshipped as the Lord" (*Comm.* Ch. 8, v. 15).

Jerome notes an interesting tradition among the Jews, "that this man who directed Gabriel to explain the vision to Daniel was Michael" (*Comm.* Ch. 8, v. 16–17). "Quite appropriately it was Gabriel, who has been put in charge of battles, to whom this duty was assigned . . . For Gabriel is translated . . . as 'the strength of' or 'the mighty one of God'" (*Comm.* Ch. 8, v. 16–17). St. Jerome uses this opportunity to teach on the other two archangels whose names are also revealed to us in Scripture. He says, "Whenever it is medicine or healing that is needed, it is Raphael who is sent, for his name is rendered as 'the healing of' or 'the medicine of God'" (*Comm.* Ch. 8, v. 16–17). Jerome continues: "When favorable promises are made to the people . . . then it is Michael who is directed to go, for his name means, 'Who is like God?' Of course the significance of the name indicates the fact that the only true remedy is to be found in God" (*Comm.* Ch. 8, v. 16–17).

Gabriel addresses Daniel as "son of man" to keep him humble and aware of his human nature. Lest his familiarity with angels cause him to puff up with pride (*Comm.* Ch. 8, v. 16–17).

At this moment, Daniel was "Overcome with terror . . . was lying on the ground face downward upon his hands and knees, but at the angel's touch he was raised up to a standing position in order that he might without perturbation attend to and understand what was spoken" (*Comm.* Ch. 8, v. 18–19). At the end of the revelation "the angel Gabriel adds . . . 'Thou therefore seal up the vision, because it shall come to pass after many days.' By the mention of a seal, he showed that the things spoken were of a hidden character and not accessible to the ears of the multitude, or susceptible of comprehension prior to their actual fulfilment by the events themselves" (*Comm.* Ch. 8, v. 26).

St. Jerome notes that the vision Daniel had was so terrifying "that he languished as a reaction to the horror of the vision, and suffered illness." But, "after he had risen from his sick-bed, he says

of lords and King of kings, was earnestly desirous of despoiling the temple of Diana which was located in Elimais, in the Persian district, because it possessed valuable votive offerings. And when he there lost his army, he was destroyed without hands, that is to say, he died of grief. As for the mention of evening and morning [in that fourteenth verse], this signifies the succession of day and night" (*Comm.* Ch. 8, v. 14).

he performed the tasks assigned to him by the king" and prefigured the Gospel principle 'Render unto Caesar the things that are Caesar's, and to God the things that are God's'; (Luke 20:25)" (*Comm.* Ch. 8, v. 27).

No one could interpret the vision because Daniel "had heard mention of kings and did not know what their names were; he learned of things to come, but he was tossed about with uncertainty as to what time they would come to pass. And so he did the only thing he could do: he marveled at the vision, and resigned everything to God's omniscience" (*Comm.* Ch. 8, v. 27).

MEDITATIO

1. Window or Mirror (continued)

If we continue to imagine this prophecy as a window that gives us a historical prophecy, we see that more details are given about the kingdoms involved. The archangel Gabriel even reveals that the "he-goat" will be the Greeks. He does not give specific names or exact times, but he gives an indication that a Greek king will arise and go against the "strength," meaning God, His people, and the Holy Temple in Jerusalem. We now know that this will be Antiochus, who inflicted horrible suffering on the Jews and sought to force the Jews to give up their religion altogether. The details of this time are recorded in the Book of the Maccabees. Antiochus was so brazen that he went as far as to erect a statue of Jupiter (Zeus) in the Temple of Jerusalem itself. He put an end to the sacrifices that were offered continuously in the Temple, and inflicted great damage on the Jewish people. But when we look at this prophecy as in a mirror, we ask again: What does this mean for us?

First, we see a dramatic encounter between Daniel and the archangel Gabriel. We do not need to search for such extraordinary encounters. The angels are with us all the time. At Mass, the priest says in the Preface to the Eucharistic Prayer, "And so, with Angels and Archangels, with Thrones and Dominions, and with all the Hosts and Powers of heaven, we sing the hymn of Your glory, as without end we acclaim: Holy, Holy, Holy Lord God of hosts." This means that at that moment at Mass, the church is filled with angels. The veil between heaven and earth becomes very thin. We ascend to heaven, and the angels descend to earth. Our worship is blended into one voice of all creation worshiping our loving God.

But the angels are with us all day, too. The Lord says that our guardian angels never sleep (Cf. Matt. 18:10). They are so devoted to the work that God has given them to lead us safely home to heaven. But do we pray to our guardian angels daily?

2. Antiochus and False Worship in the Temple of God

What can we learn from Antiochus? Antiochus would erect a pagan idol in God's Holy Temple and put an end to the sacrifices and prayers offered to God. He established his own version of religion in God's temple. We are the Temple of God. The Holy Spirit dwells in us as in a Temple. This means that I myself must become a place where continual prayers and sacrifices are offered up to God. But if I put my will above God's will, then it is like I am erecting a pagan idol in the Temple of God.

ORATIO

1. Do I seek to follow God's directives each day? Do I remember to "render unto Caesar what is Caesar, and unto God what is God's?"

2. How might I grow in devotion to the angels and especially my guardian angel?

3. Do I make sure to remember that I am a Temple of the Holy Spirit? Do I take care of myself in both body and spirit? Do I seek to be rid of all false idols and give worship only to God?

CONTEMPLATIO

LECTIO: DANIEL 9:1–7

Subject: Repentance, Collective Sin

1 In the first year of Darius the son of Assuerus of the seed of the Medes, who reigned over the kingdom of the Chaldeans: 2 The first year of his reign, I Daniel understood by books the number of the years, concerning which the word of the Lord came to Jeremias the prophet, that seventy years should be accomplished of the desolation of Jerusalem. 3 **And I set my face to the Lord my God, to pray and make supplication with fasting, and sackcloth, and ashes.** 4 And I prayed to the Lord my God, and I made my confession, and said: I beseech thee, O Lord God, great and terrible, who keepest the covenant, and mercy to them that love thee, and keep thy commandments. 5 We have sinned, we have committed iniquity, we have done wickedly, and have revolted: and we have gone aside from thy commandments, and thy judgments. 6 We have not hearkened to thy servants the prophets, that have spoken in thy name to our kings, to our princes, to our fathers, and to all the people of the land. 7 To thee, O Lord, justice: but to us confusion of face, as at this day to the men of Juda, and to the inhabitants of Jerusalem, and to all Israel to them that are near, and to them that are far off in all the countries whither thou hast driven them, for their iniquities by which they have sinned against thee.

Read with Saint Jerome

The author sets out in chapter 9 to place us in the historical time and place of the events. St. Jerome notes, "This is the Darius who in cooperation with Cyrus conquered the Chaldeans and Babylonians. We are not to think of that other Darius in the second year of whose reign the Temple was built . . . nor are we to think of the Darius who was vanquished by Alexander, the king of the Macedonians. He therefore adds the name of his father and also refers to his victory . . . He does this to avoid any mistake in the reading which might arise from the similarity of the name" (*Comm.* Ch. 9, v. 1–2).

At this time, Jeremiah had predicted seventy years for the desolation of the Temple (Jer. 52:29), at the end of which the people would again return to Judaea and build the Temple and the city of Jerusalem. It would be their homecoming. But this fact did not render Daniel careless. Rather, it encouraged him to pray that God might, through his supplications, fulfill that which He had graciously promised.

"And so it was with sackcloth and ashes that Daniel besought the Lord to fulfill what He had promised, not that Daniel lacked faith concerning the future, but rather he would avoid the danger that a feeling of security might produce carelessness, and carelessness produce an offense to God" (*Comm.* Ch. 9, v. 2). Jerome explains that when God is called "terrible" (v. 4), it means God is "terrible towards those who despise" His injunctions (*Comm.* Ch. 9, v. 4).

Although it is not Daniel's sins that have caused the exile, he takes responsibility for "the sins of the people as if he were personally guilty, on the ground of his being one of the people, just as we read the Apostle does also in his Epistle to the Romans" (*Comm.* Ch. 9, v. 5).

MEDITATIO

Set His Face

In verse 3, we read that Daniel set his face toward God. In Luke 9:51 we see a similar phrase when it says that Jesus set His face toward Jerusalem. But what does this mean exactly? To "set one's face" toward something means to turn your whole being and entire attention toward it. In Daniel's case he was devoting himself entirely to repentance and intercession on behalf of God's chosen people. He was not guilty of sin himself, but he did not stand aloof. Rather, he identified completely with the people's sins which brought them into exile in the first place. He took their sins on through intercession.

When Jesus sets His face toward Jerusalem, He is resolutely turning to the cross. He knows that the reason He has come to earth was to bring us redemption. As Bishop Fulton Sheen used to say, "We are all born to live, Jesus was born to die." He dedicated His entire being to redeeming us.

Do we ever "set our face toward God"? So often we are lukewarm in our religious observance. We give in easily to distraction, we do not seek to eliminate those things which take us away from God. We should set aside time every day to set our face toward God in prayer.

ORATIO

1. In what areas of my life am I still divided or distracted? How might I truly "set my face toward God" with my whole mind, heart, and will?

2. Do I ever grow spiritually careless because I presume on God's promises or mercy? How might more intentional repentance and discipline (like Daniel's fasting and sackcloth) renew reverence and humility in me?

3. Even when I am not personally responsible, do I take spiritual responsibility for the sins and sufferings of my community, family, or Church in prayer? Do I remain detached and distant?

CONTEMPLATIO

LECTIO: DANIEL 9:8–19

Subject: Mercy

[8] O Lord, to us belongeth confusion of face, to our princes, and
to our fathers that have sinned. [9] **But to thee, the Lord our God,
mercy and forgiveness, for we have departed from thee:** [10] And
we have not hearkened to the voice of the Lord our God, to walk
in his law, which he set before us by his servants the prophets. [11]
And all Israel have transgressed thy law, and have turned away
from hearing thy voice, and the malediction, and the curse, which
is written in the book of Moses the servant of God, is fallen upon
us, because we have sinned against him. [12] And he hath confirmed
his words which he spoke against us, and against our princes that
judged us, that he would bring in upon us a great evil, such as
never was under all the heaven, according to that which hath
been done in Jerusalem. [13] As it is written in the law of Moses, all
this evil is come upon us: and we entreated not thy face, O Lord
our God, that we might turn from our iniquities, and think on
thy truth. [14] And the Lord hath watched upon the evil, and hath
brought it upon us: the Lord our God is just in all his works which
he hath done: for we have not hearkened to his voice. [15] And now,
O Lord our God, who hast brought forth thy people out of the
land of Egypt with a strong hand, and hast made thee a name as at
this day: we have sinned, we have committed iniquity, [16] O Lord,
against all thy justice: let thy wrath and thy indignation be turned
away, I beseech thee, from thy city Jerusalem, and from thy holy
mountain. For by reason of our sins, and the iniquities of our
fathers, Jerusalem, and thy people are a reproach to all that are
round about us. [17] **Now therefore, O our God, hear the suppli-
cation of thy servant, and his prayers: and shew thy face upon
thy sanctuary which is desolate, for thy own sake.** [18] **Incline, O
my God, thy ear, and hear: open thy eyes, and see our desola-
tion, and the city upon which thy name is called: for it is not
for our justifications that we present our prayers before thy
face, but for the multitude of thy tender mercies.** [19] O Lord,
hear: O Lord, be appeased: hearken and do: delay not for thy own
sake, O my God: because thy name is invocated upon thy city, and
upon thy people.

Reading with Saint Jerome

Daniel has already said that to God belongs justice. Now he asks for mercy which is also completely in the Lord's power. So Daniel says, "'To Thee belongeth mercy.' He says this in order that he might call upon the Judge to show mercy, after His sentence has been imposed" (*Comm.* Ch. 9, v. 8).

St. Jerome notes how God has already shown mercy to the people by not pouring forth all of His just wrath, but "hast poured forth a mere droplet of [His] fury, in order that we might return unto [Him] once we have been enmeshed in His snare" (*Comm.* Ch. 9, v.11).

Regarding the blessings and curses in the law of Moses, Jerome says that it is, "In Deuteronomy (Deut. 27) we read the curses and blessings of the Lord" (Comm Ch. 9, v.11). The Israelites' obstinacy was so great that even in the midst of their toils, in exile, they would not beseech God. And, Jerome notes, "Even if they had entreated Him, it would not have been a genuine entreaty, because they had not turned back from their iniquities" (*Comm.* Ch. 9, v.13).

Whenever we are rebuked because of our sins, God is keeping watch over us and visiting us with chastisement. "But whenever we are left alone by God and we do not suffer judgment but are unworthy of the Lord's rebuke, then He is said to slumber" (*Comm.* Ch. 9, v.14). St. Jerome says that Daniel remembers God's ancient kindness in order that he may appeal to Him for a similar act of clemency (*Comm.* Ch. 9, v.15). Jerome reminds us, "This appeal is couched in anthropomorphic language, with the implication that whenever our prayers are heard, God seems to incline His ear; and whenever God deigns to have regard to us, He appears to open His eyes; but whenever He turns His face away, we appear to be unworthy of attention either from His eyes or His ears" (*Comm.* Ch. 9, v.18).

MEDITATIO

Absolute Need for Mercy

"It is not for our justifications that we present our prayers before thy face, but for the multitude of thy tender mercies" (Dan. 9:18). Daniel's prayer is radically true. We cannot justify ourselves before God. We are in absolute need of His help. The only thing that can save us is His mercy. But what is mercy? The Latin word for mercy is *misericordia* which is two words put together: *miseri*, misery and *cordia*, heart. When our misery meets the heart of Christ it is mercy that pours forth. So do not hide your misery from Him. Bring it to Him quickly! We often try to hide our misery and show God our "good side." But the truth is, we don't have a good side! Not by ourselves. We are in utter need of Him for everything. The sooner we bring our misery to Him, the sooner we experience His mercy. Blessed Columba Marmion, a spiritual writer from the twentieth-century, said, "Mercy is love in the face of misery; if there were no misery, there would be no mercy. We shall be in Heaven the living witnesses of the Divine Mercy." Marmion also said, "And what might appear astonishing, but is however very true, is that our miseries entitle us to God's mercy" (Bl. Columba Marmion, *Christ the Life of the Soul*; see also *Union with God*).

It is only our misery that gives us a right to God's mercy. What a mystery! So, what are we waiting for? Why do we try to hide our misery from Him? He is the only solution to our miserable problems. We need the childlike trust of St. Thérèse who never held anything back from Him. He sees it all already, but He wants us to willingly give Him those dark spots in our souls. He is a gentleman, He will not force His love on us. That is why He begs us to open our darkest parts, our difficult personality traits, our secret sins that no one else knows about. He is the only one who can help us. And His mercy is ours if we only ask.

ORATIO

1. Where in my life am I still trying to justify myself before God instead of honestly bringing Him my misery and trusting completely in His mercy?

2. When I experience correction, suffering, or consequences for my sins, do I recognize this as a loving rebuke meant to bring me back to Him, or do I resist and grow hardened?

3. What hidden sins, wounds, or "dark places" in my soul am I still afraid to open to God? How can I entrust them to His tender mercy with childlike trust today?

CONTEMPLATIO

LECTIO: DANIEL 9:20–27

Subject: God's Strength

20 Now while I was yet speaking, and praying, and confessing my
sins, and the sins of my people of Israel, and presenting my suppli-
cations in the sight of my God, for the holy mountain of my God:
21 As I was yet speaking in prayer, behold the man Gabriel, whom
I had seen in the vision at the beginning, flying swiftly touched
me at the time of the evening sacrifice. 22 And he instructed me,
and spoke to me, and said: O Daniel, I am now come forth to
teach thee, and that thou mightest understand. 23 **From the be-**
ginning of thy prayers the word came forth: and I am come to
shew it to thee, because thou art a man of desires: therefore
do thou mark the word, and understand the vision. 24 Seventy
weeks are shortened upon thy people, and upon thy holy city, that
transgression may be finished, and sin may have an end, and in-
iquity may be abolished; and everlasting justice may be brought;
and vision and prophecy may be fulfilled; and the saint of saints
may be anointed. 25 **Know thou therefore, and take notice: that**
from the going forth of the word, to build up Jerusalem again,
unto Christ the prince, there shall be seven weeks, and six-
ty-two weeks: and the street shall be built again, and the walls
in straitness of times. 26 **And after sixty-two weeks Christ shall**
be slain: and the people that shall deny him shall not be his.
And a people with their leader that shall come, shall destroy
the city and the sanctuary: and the end thereof shall be waste,
and after the end of the war the appointed desolation. 27 **And**
he shall confirm the covenant with many, in one week: and in
the half of the week the victim and the sacrifice shall fail: and
there shall be in the temple the abomination of desolation:
and the desolation shall continue even to the consummation,
and to the end.

Reading with Saint Jerome

We see Daniel's humility rewarded by God yet again. St. Jerome explains that "as we have pointed out above, he not only thought upon the sins of the people but also upon his own sins, as being one of the people. Or else it was by way of humility, although he had not personally committed sin; his purpose being to obtain pardon by reason of his humility" (*Comm.* Ch. 9, v.20). Another aspect to Daniel's confessing his sin could be not so much guilt as an act of praise. "There are many passages in Scripture where confession does not imply an expression of repentance so much as an expression of praise to God" (*Comm.* Ch. 9, v.20).

The Latin word for man is *vir* which is where we get the word *virtue*. Jerome therefore notes that, "Gabriel appears not as an angel or archangel, but as a man *(vir)*, a term used to indicate the quality of virtue rather than specifying his sex" (*Comm.* Ch. 9, v.21). Gabriel arrives at the time of the evening sacrifice, a note the author makes in order to show that the prophet's prayer had persisted from the morning sacrifice until the evening sacrifice. For this reason, God directed His mercy toward Daneil (*Comm.* Ch. 9, v.21).

St. Jerome interprets Gabriel's cryptic words thus: "At the time when thou didst begin to ask God, thou didst straightway obtain His mercy, and His decision was put forth. I have therefore been sent to explain to thee the things of which thou art ignorant, inasmuch as thou art a man of desires, that is to say a lovable man, worthy of God's love . . . I have been sent because thou art worthy, in recompense for thine affection for God, to be told the secret counsels of God and to have a knowledge of things to come" (*Comm.* Ch. 9, v.23).

Gabriel is the mouthpiece of God and therefore says by implication: "'By no means are they God's people, but only thy people; nor is Jerusalem the holy city of God, but it is only a holy city unto thee, as thou sayest.' This is similar to what we read in Exodus also, when God says to Moses, 'Descend, for thy people have committed sin' (Ex. 32:7). That is to say, they are not My people, for they have forsaken Me'" (*Comm.* Ch. 9, v.24–27).

And so, because of Daniel's humility and persistent pray and supplications, Gabriel, in a simple sense, tells him: "Because you are praying for Jerusalem and for the Jewish people, listen now to what will happen to your people and to your city in the months and years to come."[2]

---

[2] In his commentary on Daniel 9:24–27, Jerome refrains from adjudicating between competing patristic interpretations of the seventy weeks and instead presents the views of several major authorities, leaving judgment to the reader. Julius Africanus interprets the seventy weeks (490 years) as a literal chronological span from the twentieth year of Artaxerxes (when Nehemiah received permission to rebuild Jerusalem) to the time of Christ. He rejects Cyrus's earlier decree as the proper starting point, arguing that only under Artaxerxes did meaningful rebuilding occur. By appealing to the Hebrew lunar calendar

Gabriel reveals God's greatest strength, "when the Lord was about to be born and to declare war against the demons and to triumph over the world." For this is when, "Gabriel came to Zacharias and to Mary (Luke 1)" (*Comm.* Ch. 8, v.16–17).

---

and the system of intercalary months, Africanus harmonizes the apparent discrepancies between solar and lunar reckoning, concluding that the period indeed amounts to 490 years.

Eusebius of Caesarea offers a more complex, multi-layered interpretation. He takes seriously the deliberate division of the weeks into 7 + 62 + 1 and proposes that the "anointed princes" (christ-princes) may refer not directly to Christ, but to the successive high priests who governed Israel following the return from Babylon. The first seven weeks (49 years) correspond to the period of the Temple's reconstruction, from Cyrus to the reign of Darius, including the time of opposition and delay. The remaining sixty-two weeks trace the succession of high priests and political upheavals down to the later Hasmonean rulers and ultimately to Herod the Great, whom Eusebius views as the illegitimate, foreign usurper of Jewish authority. According to one strand of Eusebius's calculation, the 483 years (69 weeks) extend from the completion of the Temple under Darius to the reign of Herod and Augustus.

In a Christological reading of the final week, Eusebius sees the covenant confirmed "for one week" as fulfilled in Christ's public ministry, traditionally understood to last three and a half years. In the middle of this week, Christ's sacrifice renders the Temple offerings obsolete. After the Passion, Temple sacrifices continue only in appearance and not in truth. Eusebius also records an alternative tradition that stretches the final week to seventy actual years, symbolically corresponding to the period between Christ's death and the destruction of Jerusalem by the Romans under Vespasian and Titus.

Hippolytus presents yet another model, placing the first seven weeks before the return from Babylon and the sixty-two after it, but his chronology fails to match historical timelines. He interprets the final week eschatologically as the end of the world, divided between the reign of Elijah and the reign of Antichrist, during which sacrifices cease until Christ's return in judgment.

Finally, Apollinarius of Laodicea shifts the emphasis forward, confining wickedness within a 490-year span extending from Christ's birth and associating the latter part of the period with escalating conflict between the Romans and the Jews beginning in the reign of Claudius. Jerome treats this view cautiously, noting the danger of speculative chronological predictions.

Overall, Jerome's survey demonstrates both the richness and the uncertainty surrounding early Christian interpretations of Daniel's prophecy, showing it to be a focal point where chronology, messianism, ecclesiology, and eschatology all intersect.

MEDITATIO

God's Strength

St. Jerome notes that the name of Gabriel means "God's strength." This is the same Archangel Gabriel who brought God's message to Mary at the Annunciation. What a paradox. The angel called "God's strength" announces the greatest humiliation in history—God becoming man. And this is the mystery we need to wrestle with. God is breaking our human paradigms of strength and weakness. For "the weakness of God is stronger than men" (1 Cor. 1:25). He conquers our sins by His grace. He conquers our pride through His humility. He conquers our strength through His weakness. He conquers our constant rejection through His patient love (1 Cor. 13:4–7). And this is the path He has laid for us to follow. For His ways are not our ways (Is. 55:8), and "as the heavens are exalted above the earth, so are my ways exalted above your ways, and my thoughts above your thoughts" (Is. 55:9).

This mystery of strength residing in weakness is in the DNA of Christianity. The Son of God humbled Himself to become an embryo inside of Mary's womb. Is there anything weaker than a baby? But His whole life on earth was marked by weakness: He became a man, like us in all things but sin (Heb. 4:15). He learned to walk as a toddler. He got hungry and tired. He experienced all the weaknesses of human nature. And you might think this was a prelude to a triumphant victory in Jerusalem, but His victory came in the same way: His glorious strength was displayed in His inglorious and lowly passion. His divine weakness was immodestly displayed when His blood was splattered on the ground at His scourging. His kingship was announced through a public humiliation when He was crowned with thorns. And the apex of His love was the weakest a man can be—nailed immovable to a cross until death. Is there anything weaker?

But this weak and humble path is the path He laid for us to follow. And it is a path of hope. For when we are weak, then we are strong. When we are weak, then we can rely completely on His strength. When we have no human means of defending ourselves, then we can rely only on His grace. Sometimes the Lord removes our crutches so that we lean only on Him. And then we can truly say, "I please myself in my infirmities, in reproaches, in necessities, in persecutions, in distresses, for Christ. For when I am weak, then am I powerful" (2 Cor. 12:10).

ORATIO

1. Do I approach God with true humility, admitting my sin and need for mercy, or do I still try to justify myself?

2. How is God inviting me to accept weakness, suffering, or humiliation as a path to His strength and grace?

3. In what areas of my life is Christ calling me to trust His power more than my own?

CONTEMPLATIO

LECTIO: DANIEL 10:1–3

Subject: Fasting, Penance, and Encounter with God

1 **In the third year of Cyrus king of the Persians, a word was
revealed to Daniel surnamed Baltasar, and a true word, and
great strength: and he understood the word: for there is need
of understanding in a vision.** 2 In those days I Daniel mourned
the days of three weeks. 3 I ate no desirable bread, and neither
flesh, nor wine entered into my mouth, neither was I anointed
with ointment: till the days of three weeks were accomplished.

Reading with Saint Jerome

Like much of the book of Daniel, prophetic vision is placed within historical context. Here, St. Jerome aims to date the timing of this vision. "We understand that [Daniel] enjoyed his former high position among the Chaldeans, right up until the first year of King Cyrus, when Cyrus overthrew the Chaldeans, and afterwards Daniel commenced service under Darius, the son of Ahasuerus of the Median line, who reigned over the kingdom of the Chaldeans. Or else that Darius had already died . . . and he is now relating that he beheld these things in the third year of King Cyrus" (*Comm.* Ch. 10, v.1).

St. Jerome explains that the "true word and great strength" "refers either to the strength of the God who was going to perform these things or to the strength of the prophet who would comprehend them" (*Comm.* Ch. 10, v.1). Daniel's fasting teaches us to abstain from the pleasanter types of food as a means of purifying ourselves and growing in holiness, of which Jerome was a major proponent. "Daniel afflicted his soul for three consecutive weeks, so that his intercession might not appear cursory or casual" (*Comm.* Ch. 10, v.2–3).

Here, Jerome draws out a further spiritual meaning for fasting, noting that, "A person in mourning who bemourns the absence of one betrothed partakes of no desirable bread though it comes down from heaven itself . . . nor does he drink any wine, which gladdens the heart of man . . . By means of such a fast as this the betrothed girl sheds tears . . . when her fiancé has been taken from her" (*Comm.* Ch. 10, v.2–3). Daniel's three weeks of mourning and fasting was more than an act of self-denial. It was the bodily expression of an interior hunger, a longing for God, for truth, and for the fulfillment of His promises. In a way, his fasting and mourning become a school of love. His body preaches what his lips cannot—that God alone is enough, and that every other joy is a shadow compared to Him.

MEDITATIO

It is not exactly clear why Daniel was mourning and fasting, but if we follow the whole narrative, we see that after his fasting, he had a dramatic encounter of divine revelation. From this we can draw out that for us, fasting and penance are a preparation for prayer and encounter with God.

How does fasting and penance prepare us for prayer? First, we must always remember that we are body-soul creatures. We are not pure spirits like the angels, nor are we souls trapped in a body like Plato believed. Everything that we do, we do as body-soul persons. Our bodies matter in our spiritual life. We kneel, stand, and sit in order to dispose ourselves at Mass to encounter God. But it is not merely our soul that kneels—our soul doesn't even have knees! *We* kneel because we are body and soul. Fasting and penance help to align our body with our soul in our search for intimacy with God.

To lose weight, we often go on a diet. And while that is not the reason for spiritual fasting, it still tells us something true: We fast because there is *too much me*. My ego and self-will are bloated. We fast in order to tell ourself "you can't always get what you want." Giving up food or drink is a small act to wrestle our bodily desires into submission. We need this more than ever today. We have a superabundance of access to all kinds of food and consumables; we get what we want whenever we want it. But as the *Catechism* tells us, "Fasting and penance prepare us for prayer and hearing God's Word" (*CCC* 1434). We need to employ fasting as a more deliberate act to learn how to say no to our desires, to align body with spirit, and prepare for union with God.

But fasting can't be just about us. It needs to move us outside ourselves to something else. Jesus gives us a direction and intention for our fasting. He tells us that His disciples will fast and mourn when the bridegroom is taken away from them. This is us. The Lord has ascended and removed Himself from our physical eyes. We need to employ our body in fasting for our Bridegroom. We await His return in glory, and we should prepare ourselves. A bride will usually prepare herself for her wedding day by going to the gym and dieting, perhaps. We stand as the bride of Christ awaiting our His return. We should make a habit of dieting our wills through fasting, that He might be pleased with us on our wedding day.

ORATIO

1. Where in my life is there "too much me"? What might I fast from to get back into alignment with God?

2. When I fast or give something up, am I doing it merely out of discipline or as an expression of love and longing for my Bridegroom?

3. How is God inviting me right now to use my body (through prayer, posture, self-denial, or silence) to prepare more deeply for an encounter with Him?

CONTEMPLATIO

LECTIO: DANIEL 10:4–9

Subject: Fear of the Lord

4 And in the four and twentieth day of the first month I was by the
great river which is the Tigris. 5 And I lifted up my eyes, and I saw:
and behold a man clothed in linen, and his loins were girded with
the finest gold: 6 And his body was like the chrysolite, and his face
as the appearance of lightning, and his eyes as a burning lamp: and
his arms, and all downward even to the feet, like in appearance
to glittering brass: and the voice of his word like the voice of a
multitude. 7 **And I Daniel alone saw the vision: for the men that**
were with me saw it not: but an exceeding great terror fell upon
them, and they fled away, and hid themselves. 8 **And I being**
left alone saw this great vision: and there remained no strength
in me, and the appearance of my countenance was changed in
me, and I fainted away, and retained no strength. 9 **And I heard**
the voice of his words: and when I heard, I lay in a consterna-
tion, upon my face, and my face was close to the ground.

Reading with Saint Jerome

The prophet describes an overwhelming vision beside the great river Tigris. Lifting his eyes, Daniel sees a mysterious figure clothed in linen, girded with fine gold. The figure's dazzling appearance (body like chrysolite, face like lightning, eyes like burning lamps, and limbs like gleaming brass) reveals a being whose glory surpasses anything earthly. The power of the sight is so immense that Daniel's companions flee in terror, while Daniel himself collapses, losing all strength and falling face-down in awe and fear.

Reading this passage, St. Jerome immediately connects Daniel's experience to other sacred moments by rivers. "Ezekiel also had seen a great vision beside a river, the Chebar (Ez. 1). And it was by the stream of the Jordan that the heavens were opened to the gaze of our Lord and Savior and also to John the Baptist (Matt. 3)" (*Comm.* Ch. 10, v.4). Rivers thus appear as thresholds of divine revelation. Just as physical elevation is needed to see clearly, Jerome insists on spiritual readiness: "We must lift up our eyes if we are to be able to discern a mystical vision" (*Comm.* Ch. 10, v.5).

Although Daniel describes the figure as a man, Jerome clarifies that this was not an ordinary human presence, but "'One like unto a man,' inasmuch as he was not actually a man but only had the appearance of one." Even the detail of chrysolite carries sacred significance, since it was "one of the twelve gems inserted in the oracular breastplate of the high priest" (*Comm.* Ch. 10, v.6).

Daniel alone receives the vision, a pattern Jerome likens to St. Paul, who was granted a private revelation while others perceived nothing: "In the Book of Acts, in that while the others could see nothing, [Paul] alone beheld the vision (Acts 22)" (*Comm.* Ch. 10, v.7). In this moment, Daniel becomes both witness and participant in the terrifying holiness of God's revealed mystery.

MEDITATIO

Fear of the Lord

This naked encounter shows Daniel's spontaneous reaction to the divine. He falls facedown to the ground. This is not premeditated, but is the cry of his heart. He simply cannot boast before God or pretend to be strong in His midst. Too often we wear a mask of strength, as if we can possibly stand before God.

This encounter reveals the gift of the Holy Spirit that is called the "Fear of the Lord." Archbishop Luis Martinez describes three levels to the gift of "Fear of the Lord": Servile fear, filial fear, and reverential fear. We have seen before how our spiritual life must grow from a *fear* of God to *love* of God, but the gift of "Fear of the Lord" remains in us always. Not only is it the beginning of wisdom as the Psalm says, but even the saints and angels are imbued with this reverential fear in heaven. It is a deeply infused awareness of God as creator and ourselves as creature. St. Catherine of Siena experienced this in a radical way when Jesus appeared to her and said, "I am HE WHO IS and you are she who is not." Because this knowledge is deep and interior, breathed into us by the Holy Spirit, we spontaneously throw ourselves at His feet. It is as if all our masks have been torn away and we stand before Him as He is and as we are.

ORATIO

1. Am I still trying to "stand strong" or maintain control before God instead of allowing myself to be humbled and undone in His presence?

2. Where in my spiritual life is "Fear of the Lord" strong? Where has it been replaced by familiarity, distraction, or self-reliance?

3. What masks is God asking me to lay down so that I can stand honestly before Him as I truly am?

CONTEMPLATIO

LECTIO: DANIEL 10:10–15

Subject: Perseverance in Prayer

10 And behold a hand touched me, and lifted me up upon my knees, and upon the joints of my hands. 11 **And he said to me: Daniel, thou man of desires, understand the words that I speak to thee, and stand upright: for I am sent now to thee. And when he had said this word to me, I stood trembling.** 12 **And he said to me: Fear not, Daniel: for from the first day that thou didst set thy heart to understand, to afflict thyself in the sight of thy God, thy words have been heard: and I am come for thy words.** 13 But the prince of the kingdom of the Persians resisted me one and twenty days: and behold Michael, one of the chief princes, came to help me, and I remained there by the king of the Persians. 14 But I am come to teach thee what things shall befall thy people in the latter days, for as yet the vision is for days. 15 And when he was speaking such words to me, I cast down my countenance to the ground, and held my peace.

Reading with Saint Jerome

Daniel's encounter with the heavenly messenger reveals both God's gentleness and the invisible spiritual warfare at work behind human history. After Daniel collapses in fear and weakness, "The angel appeared in the form of a man and laid his hand upon the human prophet as he lay upon the ground, in order that he might not be terrified" (*Comm.* Ch. 10, v.10). In a gesture of paternal care, the angel strengthens Daniel physically and spiritually, addressing him as one beloved by God. Jerome explains, "It was fitting that [Daniel] be addressed as a man of desires, for by . . . urgent prayer and affliction of body and the discipline of severe fasting he desired to learn of the future and to be informed of the secret counsels of God" (*Comm.* Ch. 10, v.11).

Although Daniel's prayer was heard immediately, its visible answer was delayed: "On the twenty-fourth day of the first month . . . after three weeks had elapsed [Daniel] beheld this vision, and he heard from the angel that on the very first day he had begun to pray and to afflict himself before God, his words had been heard and granted" (*Comm.* Ch. 10, v.12). Jerome teaches that "by reason of the delay an opportunity was afforded him of praying to the

Lord at greater length, so that in proportion as his earnest desire was intensified, he might by his effort the more fully deserve to hear" (*Comm.* Ch. 10, v.12). The angel clarifies: "After thou didst begin to invoke God's mercy by good works and tearful supplication and fasting, then I for my part embraced the opportunity of entering in before God and praying for thee" (*Comm.* Ch. 10, v.12).

The mysterious resistance of the "Prince of Persia" reveals the reality of angelic governance: "In my opinion [the Prince of Persia] was the angel to whose charge Persia was committed" (*Comm.* Ch. 10, v.13). These are "the princes" of whom St. Paul speaks. Jerome explains, "And so the prince or angel of the Persians offered resistance" until Michael intervened: "By chief princes we are of course to understand archangels." Ultimately, the angel comes to reveal "what is going to happen to the people of Israel . . . in the last days" (*Comm.* Ch. 10, v.13–14).

MEDITATIO

"From the first day . . . thy words have been heard."

This is such a difficult and yet utterly hopeful passage. The angel tells Daniel that as soon as he undertook his spiritual practice and set his heart on God, the Lord heard him. At the very moment Daniel started fasting, God responded with an attentive ear. There is no delay in God's response with regard to hearing our prayer. Yet we immediately think of the situations in our life where God not only seems to delay, but to ignore our pleas altogether. How do we make sense of this?

In Daniel's case, he did not know God had heard him for three weeks. To some of us, in certain situations, three weeks can feel like a lifetime. But Daniel prayed and fasted nonetheless. Three weeks may not sound like very long, but it is not the length of time that matters most. Rather, it is the posture of faith. Daniel persevered in prayer even without any assurance or emotional confirmation that God was listening. This is how we must learn to pray.

And yet, we actually have more assurance than Daniel ever did, for Christ Himself has said, "I am with you always" and "Whatever you ask in my name will be given you." Still, our hearts must be shaped and purified before such gifts can be received.

But why does God delay? St. Augustine says, "God does not delay to hear our prayers because He has no mind to give; but that by enlarging our desires, He may give us more largely" (Letter 130). God is stretching the heart to increase its capacity. He has so much to give, but we are often too small to receive it. And so

He makes us wait, not to withhold His goodness, but to make us capable of it.

ORATIO

1. When I feel like God is silent, do I still persevere in prayer and sacrifice like Daniel, or do I give up when I don't see immediate results on my timeline?

2. In what ways might God be using this "delay" in my life to enlarge my desires and stretch my heart to receive more of Him?

3. What spiritual practice (fasting, silence, self-denial, perseverance in prayer) is God inviting me to embrace more deeply so that my heart can be better aligned with His will?

CONTEMPLATIO

LECTIO: DANIEL 10:16–21

Subject: God's Attentiveness

16 And behold, as it were the likeness of a son of man touched my
lips: then I opened my mouth, and spoke, and said to him that
stood before me: O my lord, at the sight of thee my joints are
loosed, and no strength hath remained in me. 17 And how can the
servant of my lord speak with my lord? for no strength remaineth
in me, moreover my breath is stopped. 18 Therefore he that looked
like a man touched me again, and strengthened me. 19 **And he**
said: Fear not, O man of desires, peace be to thee: take courage
and be strong. And when he spoke to me, I grew strong: and I
said: Speak, O my lord, for thou hast strengthened me. 20 **And**
he said: Dost thou know wherefore I am come to thee? and
now I will return, to fight against the prince of the Persians.
When I went forth, there appeared the prince of the Greeks
coming. 21 **But I will tell thee what is set down in the scripture**
of truth: and none is my helper in all these things, but Michael
your prince.

Reading with Saint Jerome

The prophet is strengthened through a divine touch and invited once more into the mystery of God's plan, yet not without trembling before its glory. St. Jerome connects the phrase "his joints were loosed" with Psalm 102:3, offering a profound interior reading of the moment. "Our inward nature must direct its gaze without, before we deserve to behold a vision of God; and when we actually have beheld a vision of God, then our inward nature is converted within us" (*Comm.* Ch. 10, v.16). In other words, God's revelation first unsettles, then purifies, and finally reorients the soul toward Himself, much like the moments of spiritual union: purgation to illumination to union.

Jerome emphasizes that Daniel could not have endured this revelation had the angel not comforted him. Unless he had been reassured "by touching him so that his heart was freed of terror, he would not have been able to hearken to God's secrets" (*Comm.* Ch. 10, v.19). Divine truth is therefore not only revealed, but mercy accompanies it, strengthening human frailty.

The angel's mission is further clarified when he says, "I myself was departing from God's presence in order to announce to thee . . . the events which are to befall thy people in the last days" (*Comm.* Ch. 10, v.20). Jerome reflects on the mysterious mention of the princes of Persia and Greece. Though difficult to interpret, these "princes" are understood as angelic guardians of nations engaged in a providential unfolding of history. "And behold, the prince of the Greeks . . . entered in before God's presence . . . so that the prince of the Greeks did overcome the prince of the Persians" (*Comm.* Ch. 10, v.21), a reality later mirrored in Alexander's conquest.

The angel also reminds Daniel of heavenly intercession: "I am that angel who presents thy prayers to God . . . except the archangel Michael, to whose charge the Jewish nation has been entrusted" (*Comm.* Ch. 10, v.21). Thus, this passage unveils not only God's sovereignty over history, but His loving use of angelic ministry in guiding and defending His people.

MEDITATIO

God's Attentiveness

Daniel's encounter with the "Son of Man" bears the mark of a mystical meeting with the pre-incarnate Christ. Though the Lord had not yet taken flesh, the plan of the Incarnation was eternal, and He already revealed Himself in anticipation of that mystery. This vision teaches us first and foremost that we are entirely dependent upon grace. Daniel is unable even to speak until he is touched. Only then are his lips opened. How different this is from our ordinary habits of prayer, in which we rush to speak without first acknowledging the presence of the Creator and Redeemer before whom we stand. Daniel's silence is instructive. It echoes the beginning of the Divine Office of the Church: "Lord, open my lips, and my mouth will proclaim your praise." True prayer begins not with our words, but with God's action.

When Daniel finally speaks, his first words are a confession of weakness. His breath is taken away. His strength fails him. In this, he becomes a living witness to the truth St. Paul later expresses: "We do not know how to pray as we ought," and so "the Spirit Himself intercedes for us with inexpressible groanings" (Rom. 8:26). Daniel's emptiness creates space for God's strength. The Son of Man touches him again, not to overwhelm him, but to strengthen him. Prayer becomes a true dialogue: human weakness answered by divine grace.

Then comes the familiar heavenly assurance: "Fear not . . . peace be with thee." The Lord does not desire that we remain crushed by our frailty. Rather, He enters into it. As Daniel listens to the words spoken to him, he "grows strong." We too are strengthened not by our own effort alone, but by "every word that comes from the mouth of God" (Matt. 4:4). The flesh is of no avail, but the Spirit gives life (John 6:63). In prayer, it is God Himself who supplies what we lack, forming us, sustaining us, and drawing us ever closer to Himself.

ORATIO

1. When I pray and don't see an immediate answer, do I still trust that God has already heard me?

2. How can I practice the same persistence and faithfulness in prayer that Daniel showed, even without reassurance?

3. To I take time in prayer to first listen, then give praise to God? Do I allow the Holy Spirit to strengthen and lead me?

CONTEMPLATIO

LECTIO: DANIEL 11:1–4

SUBJECT: DIVISION AND THE DIABOLIC

1 And from the first year of Darius the Mede I stood up that he
might be strengthened and confirmed. 2 **And now I will shew**
thee the truth. Behold there shall stand yet three kings in Per-
sia, and the fourth shall be enriched exceedingly above them
all: and when he shall be grown mighty by his riches, he shall stir
up all against the kingdom of Greece. 3 But there shall rise up a
strong king, and shall rule with great power: and he shall do what
he pleaseth. 4 **And when he shall come to his height, his king-**
dom shall be broken, and it shall be divided towards the four
winds of the heaven: but not to his posterity, nor according to
his power with which he ruled. For his kingdom shall be rent
in pieces, even for strangers, beside these.

READING WITH SAINT JEROME

The angel reveals that God governs the rise and fall of earthly kingdoms according to His providential plan. The passage announces a succession of Persian kings, followed by a mighty ruler whose empire will collapse and be divided. The focus is not mere political history, but divine sovereignty over time and nations.

St. Jerome explains Daniel's concern for Darius, writing, "Daniel implies, 'From the first year of the reign of Darius, who overthrew the Chaldeans and delivered me from the hand of my enemies . . . and I besought God's mercy upon him . . . in order that either he or his kingdom might be strengthened and confirmed'" (*Comm.* Ch. 11, v.1). This reveals Daniel's intercessory heart and gratitude toward the ruler who freed him.

Jerome identifies the kings named in the prophecy, explaining that "Four kings shall arise in Persia after Cyrus . . . and by him [Darius] gave birth to Xerxes, who became a most powerful and wealthy king, and led an innumerable host against Greece" (*Comm.* Ch. 11, v.2). He notes that another writer "is in error . . . for he was not the fourth king, but the fourteenth king of the Persians after Cyrus." Jerome adds, "the Spirit of prophecy was not concerned about preserving historical detail but in summarizing only the most important matters" (*Comm.* Ch. 11, v. 3).

The "strong king" is "Clearly Alexander the Great" (*Comm.* Ch. 11, v.3–4), who conquered vast territories and died young. After him, "his kingdom was divided towards the four winds" among Ptolemy, Philip, Seleucus, and Antigonus (*Comm.* Ch. 11, v.3–4). Jerome explains, "'But not unto his own posterity,' [means] Alexander would have no children, but rather, his kingdom would be rent asunder and fall to others" and further fragmented among "petty kings" and provinces (*Comm.* Ch. 11, v.3–4). Ultimately, Daniel's vision reminds us that all human power is fleeting, and only God's kingdom endures.

MEDITATIO

Division and the Diabolic

Scripture tells us that Alexander's kingdom would be "rent into pieces," divided toward the four winds. Our Lord Himself teaches, "If a kingdom be divided against itself, that kingdom cannot stand . . . and if Satan be risen up against himself, he is divided, and cannot stand, but hath an end" (Mark 3:24–26). The fragmenting of earthly empires is more than a political reality; it points to a deeper, spiritual truth about the nature of division.

God is not division, but communion. He is a perfect unity of love—Father, Son, and Holy Spirit—and His plan from the beginning has been to "reunite all things in Christ" (cf. Eph. 1:10). The devil's rebellion was precisely a rejection of this communion. The word diabolic comes from *diabolos*, meaning "to divide" or "to separate." In seeking a kingdom apart from God, Satan introduced fractures where there was unity, beginning with the angels and then with humanity in the garden.

Every earthly kingdom that is not rooted in God's order will, in some way, bear the mark of this division. Alexander's empire, for all its splendor, could not endure because it was founded on human power rather than divine communion.

This truth confronts us personally: Where do we see division in our own life—within our hearts, families, parishes, or communities? Such wounds cannot be healed by our effort alone. They require grace. We must be wary of aligning ourselves with anything that sows discord, especially within the Church. Instead, we are called to cooperate with God's healing work, asking Him to restore unity and to draw us ever more deeply into the communion for which we were created.

ORATIO

1. Where do I see division at work in my own heart, and how might I be contributing to it rather than healing it?

2. What "kingdoms" in my life (ambitions, loyalties, attachments) am I placing ahead of God's communion and unity?

3. How is the Lord inviting me to become an instrument of reconciliation and unity in my family, parish, or community?

CONTEMPLATIO

LECTIO: DANIEL 11:5–20

SUBJECT: OBEDIENCE, GOD'S PLAN

[5] **And the king of the south shall be strengthened, and one of
his princes shall prevail over him, and he shall rule with great
power: for his dominion shall be great.** [6] And after the end of
years they shall be in league together: and the daughter of the king
of the south shall come to the king of the north to make friend-
ship, but she shall not obtain the strength of the arm, neither shall
her seed stand: and she shall be given up, and her young men that
brought her, and they that strengthened her in these times. [7] And
a plant of the bud of her roots, shall stand up: and he shall come
with an army, and shall enter into the province of the king of the
north: and he shall abuse them, and shall prevail. [8] And he shall
also carry away captive into Egypt their gods, and their graven
things, and their precious vessels of gold and silver: he shall prevail
against the king of the north. [9] And the king of the south shall
enter into the kingdom, and shall return to his own land. [10] And
his sons shall be provoked, and they shall assemble a multitude
of great forces: and he shall come with haste like a flood: and he
shall return and be stirred up, and he shall join battle with his
forces. [11] And the king of the south being provoked shall go forth,
and shall fight against the king of the north, and shall prepare an
exceeding great multitude, and a multitude shall be given into
his hand. [12] And he shall take a multitude, and his heart shall be
lifted up, and he shall cast down many thousands: but he shall not
prevail. [13] For the king of the north shall return and shall prepare
a multitude much greater than before: and in the end of times and
years, he shall come in haste with a great army, and much rich-
es. [14] And in those times many shall rise up against the king of the
south, and the children of prevaricators of thy people shall lift up
themselves to fulfill the vision, and they shall fall. [15] And the king
of the north shall come, and shall cast up a mount, and shall take
the best fenced cities: and the arms of the south shall not with-
stand, and his chosen ones shall rise up to resist, and they shall not
have strength. [16] And he shall come upon him and do according
to his pleasure, and there shall be none to stand against his face:
and he shall stand in the glorious land, and it shall be consumed
by his hand. [17] And he shall set his face to come to possess all his

kingdom, and he shall make upright conditions with him: and
he shall give him a daughter of women, to overthrow it: and she
shall not stand, neither shall she be for him. 18 And he shall turn
his face to the islands, and shall take many: and he shall cause the
prince of his reproach to cease, and his reproach shall be turned
upon him. 19 And he shall turn his face to the empire of his own
land, and he shall stumble, and fall, and shall not be found. 20 And
there shall stand up in his place, one most vile, and unworthy of
kingly honour: and in a few days he shall be destroyed, not in rage
nor in battle.

Read with Saint Jerome

This passage is detailed and cryptic in its historical nature, but St. Jerome helps us understand the conflicts between the kings of the North and South, primarily the Seleucid and Ptolemaic dynasties, in relation to Judaea. Jerome explains, "The king of the South refers to Ptolemy, son of Lagos, who was the first to become king in Egypt, and was a very clever, mighty and wealthy man . . . But no further notice is taken of the other kingdoms . . . because Judaea lay in a midway position and was held now by one group of kings and now by another" (*Comm.* Ch.11, v.5). The Scripture focuses not on general history but on events affecting Israel: "It is not the purpose of Holy Scripture to cover external history apart from the Jews, but only that which is linked up with the nation of Israel" (*Comm.* Ch.11, v.5).

The passage narrates the marriage of Berenice, daughter of Ptolemy Philadelphus, to Antiochus Theos of the North, intended to secure peace. Jerome notes that despite the political union, she "will not be able to gain her end, nor shall her posterity remain upon the throne of Syria, but instead both Berenice and the men who had escorted her thither shall be put to death" (*Comm.* Ch.11, v.6). Later, her brother Ptolemy Euergetes invades Syria to assert control, seizing territory and valuable spoils, yet ultimately, human ambition cannot fully prevail. Antiochus the Great retaliates, while Judaea suffers from factional division, illustrating how foreign powers impact God's chosen people.

Jerome also highlights a hopeful development: "Finally the high priest, Onias, fled to Egypt, taking a large number of Jews along with him, and was given by Ptolemy an honorable reception . . . he erected a temple in Egypt like the temple of the Jews . . . fulfilling the prophecy written by Isaiah: 'There shall be an altar of the Lord in Egypt, and the name of the Lord shall be found in their territories'" (*Comm.* Ch.11, v.13–14).

Ultimately, the "glorious land" (Jerusalem and Judaea) remains central: "And as for the statement, 'And he shall stand in the glorious land, and it shall be consumed by his hand,' signifies Judaea, and particularly Jerusalem" (*Comm.* Ch.11, v.15–16). The passage further emphasizes that human ambition and dynastic strife are subordinate to God's providential plan for His people.

MEDITATIO

Obedience and Building Our House on Rock

Daniel gives us many details about the kings and kingdoms who are to come. He gives us a sneak peak of how they will wage war, create alliances, rise and fall leading up to Antiochus. St. Jerome reminds us that although these kingdoms relate true history, they nonetheless are more properly understood as a type or prefigurement of the Antichrist and what will come upon the Church in the last days.

Yet there is meaning for us here and now. If we look at the rise and fall of these kingdoms alongside the teaching of Jesus, we find important lessons for our spiritual life.

At the end of the sermon on the mount, after giving his new interpretation of the law, Jesus says, "Every one therefore that heareth these my words, and doth them, shall be likened to a wise man that built his house upon a rock, And the rain fell, and the floods came, and the winds blew, and they beat upon that house, and it fell not, for it was founded on a rock" (Matt. 7:21–27). The kingdoms Daniel relates were built on sand because they were not founded on the Word of God.

How, then, do we build our life on rock? By "hearing and doing" the word of Christ. First, we must truly hear the word. Too often we exercise a shallow hearing, but we need to *listen* deeply. The word obedience comes from the Latin verb *audire,* "to listen" and the prefix *ob*, which means "deep." To be obedient to the word is not a mindless slavishness. It means first a profound listening; hearing deeply and allowing God's word to penetrate us. We need to take His word deeply into our hearts, so that we can be formed and reformed. Only then can we become doers of the word. We cannot live it out, give it away, and put it into action unless we are first transformed by His words. And this requires true obedience, *listening deeply.*

ORATIO

1. Do I truly listen to God's Word? In what ways might my hearing be shallow or distracted?

2. What in my life is "built on sand"? How can I rebuild them upon the rock of Christ's Word?

3. How can I move from simply hearing Scripture to actively doing it in my daily choices and relationships?

CONTEMPLATIO

LECTIO: DANIEL 11:21–35

Subject: The Antichrist and Victory of Christ

21 And there shall stand up in his place one despised, and the kingly honour shall not be given him: and he shall come privately, and shall obtain the kingdom by fraud. 22 And the arms of the fighter shall be overcome before his face, and shall be broken; yea also the prince of the covenant. 23 And after friendships, he will deal deceitfully with him: and he shall go up, and shall overcome with a small people. 24 And he shall enter into rich and plentiful cities: and he shall do that which his fathers never did, nor his fathers' fathers: he shall scatter their spoils, and their prey, and their riches, and shall forecast devices against the best fenced places: and this until a time. 25 And his strength and his heart shall be stirred up against the king of the south with a great army: and the king of the south shall be stirred up to battle with many and very strong succours: and they shall not stand, for they shall form designs against him. 26 And they that eat bread with him, shall destroy him, and his army shall be overthrown: and many shall fall down slain. 27 And the heart of the two kings shall be to do evil, and they shall speak lies at one table, and they shall not prosper: because as yet the end is unto another time. 28 And he shall return into his land with much riches: and his heart shall be against the holy covenant, and he shall succeed and shall return into his own land. 29 At the time appointed he shall return, and he shall come to the south, but the latter time shall not be like the former. 30 And the galleys and the Romans shall come upon him, and he shall be struck, and shall return, and shall have indignation against the covenant of the sanctuary, and he shall succeed: and he shall return and shall devise against them that have forsaken the covenant of the sanctuary. 31 **And arms shall stand on his part, and they shall defile the sanctuary of strength, and shall take away the continual sacrifice, and they shall place there the abomination unto desolation.** 32 **And such as deal wickedly against the covenant shall deceitfully dissemble: but the people that know their God shall prevail and succeed.** 33 **And they that are learned among the people shall teach many: and they shall fall by the sword, and by fire, and by captivity, and by spoil for many days.** 34 **And when they shall have fallen they shall be**

relieved with a small help: and many shall be joined to them deceitfully. [35] **And some of the learned shall fall, that they may be tried, and may be chosen, and made white even to the appointed time, because yet there shall be another time.**

Reading with Saint Jerome

In these verses the prophet describes the rise of a contemptible king, his deceitful strategies, and persecution of the covenant, which St. Jerome interprets both historically and prophetically. Jerome notes, "Up to this point the historical order has been followed . . . But the rest of the text he interprets as applying to the person of the Antiochus who was surnamed Epiphanes. It is under his reign that the persecution of God's Law is related, and also the wars of the Maccabees" (*Comm.* Ch.11, v.24). Yet Jerome emphasizes, "But those of our persuasion believe all these things are spoken prophetically of the Antichrist who is to arise in the end time" (*Comm.* Ch.11, v.24). Antiochus serves as a type of the Antichrist, prefiguring the ultimate persecution of God's people.

Jerome explains that the "abomination of desolation" and the oppression described in the Maccabees were preliminary fulfillments, pointing forward to the Antichrist, who will arise deceptively, oppose the holy covenant, and test the faithful (*Comm.* Ch.11, v.31–33). The faithful, "the people who know their God," shall prevail through endurance and fidelity, even amidst suffering and persecution (Dan 11:32). Jerome stresses that God allows these trials to refine the saints, making them "white and chosen out, until the time before determined arrives," with ultimate victory coming only at the Second Coming of Christ (*Comm.* Ch.11, v.34–35).

Through this passage, Daniel teaches both historical and spiritual lessons. Antiochus's cunning and oppression foreshadow the spiritual struggle believers will face under the Antichrist, while the endurance of the Maccabees models fidelity to God's law. The faithful are called to remain steadfast, trusting in God's providence, and to be purified through trials so that their hearts and lives are firmly founded on Christ. In this way, the prophecy encourages perseverance, hope, and the deepening of obedience to God's covenant.

MEDITATIO

Antichrist and Welcoming Christ

"We hold that it is the habit of Holy Scripture to set forth by means of types the reality of things to come . . . the Antichrist very properly had as a type of himself the utterly wicked king, Antiochus, who persecuted the saints and defiled the Temple" (*Comm.* Ch.11, v.24). St. Jerome shows us that while the events described in Daniel were fulfilled under Antiochus, they also prefigure the Antichrist, who will arise at the end of time. The little horn of Daniel points toward this ultimate opposition to Christ.

But who is the Antichrist? The word Christ means "the anointed one," so the Antichrist is one who stands against the Anointed. The Church teaches that at the end of time, an earthly ruler will arise in great opposition to Jesus. Yet the Antichrist is not only a distant figure—anyone who denies that Christ has come in the flesh embodies this evil nature: "For many seducers are gone out into the world, who confess not that Jesus Christ is come in the flesh: this is a seducer and an antichrist" (2 John 1:7). Faith in the true humanity of Jesus is essential, for His Incarnation is the Way to God.

We are called not to treat the Antichrist as abstract speculation but to recognize the opposition to Christ in our lives and culture. The antidote is to welcome the Incarnation as Mary did. At the Annunciation, she said yes and became *Theotokos*, the God-bearer. Our Lord calls us to follow her example: "The one who welcomes the word and does it will be my mother." Like Mary, we must allow Christ to dwell in us, transforming our hearts and bodies into His. In the Eucharist, we receive Christ truly in the flesh; we must welcome Him with Mary's same openness, letting Him take root in our lives. Only then can we bring Christ to others, becoming little God-bearers, witnesses of the Gospel, and living icons of His presence.

ORATIO

1. How do I actively welcome the Incarnation of Christ in my daily life, as our Blessed Mother welcomed Him at the Annunciation?

2. Where do I encounter the "spirit of the Antichrist" today—through attitudes, ideas, or actions that deny or diminish Christ's true humanity—and how can I resist it?

3. How can receiving the Eucharist with Mary's openness transform my heart and enable me to become a witness of Christ to others?

CONTEMPLATIO

LECTIO: DANIEL 11: 36–45

Subject: Divine Judgment, Christ's Victory

36 **And the king shall do according to his will, and he shall**
be lifted up, and shall magnify himself against every god: and
he shall speak great things against the God of gods, and shall
prosper, till the wrath be accomplished. For the determination
is made. 37 **And he shall make no account of the God of his**
fathers: and he shall follow the lust of women, and he shall not
regard any gods: for he shall rise up against all things. 38 But
he shall worship the god Maozim in his place: and a god whom
his fathers knew not, he shall worship with gold, and silver, and
precious stones, and things of great price. 39 And he shall do this
to fortify Maozim with a strange god, whom he hath acknowl-
edged, and he shall increase glory and shall give them power over
many, and shall divide the land gratis. 40 And at the time prefixed
the king of the south shall fight against him, and the king of the
north shall come against him like a tempest, with chariots, and
with horsemen, and with a great navy, and he shall enter into the
countries, and shall destroy, and pass through. 41 And he shall en-
ter into the glorious land, and many shall fall: and these only shall
be saved out of his hand, Edom, and Moab, and the principality
of the children of Ammon. 42 **And he shall lay his hand upon the**
lands: and the land of Egypt shall not escape. 43 **And he shall**
have power over the treasures of gold, and of silver, and all the
precious things of Egypt: and he shall pass through Libya, and
Ethiopia. 44 **And tidings out of the east, and out of the north**
shall trouble him: and he shall come with a great multitude to
destroy and slay many. 45 **And he shall fix his tabernacle Apad-**
no between the seas, upon a glorious and holy mountain: and
he shall come even to the top thereof, and none shall help him.

Reading with Saint Jerome

St. Jerome continues his analysis of Daniel's prophecy, observing that the events described under Antiochus Epiphanes prefigure the Antichrist: "The Jews believe that this passage has reference to the Antichrist . . . We too understand this to refer to the Antichrist. But Porphyry . . . suppose the reference to be to Antiochus Epiphanes, pointing out that he did raise himself up against the worship of God, and . . . commanded his own statue to be set up in the Temple in Jerusalem" (*Comm.* Ch.11, v.36).

Jerome distinguishes between the historical fulfillment in Antiochus and the prophetic reality awaiting the Antichrist. "And as for the subsequent statement, 'And he shall manage successfully until the wrath be accomplished, for the consummation shall be in him,' we maintain that even though this thing befell him, it did so because he had perpetrated great cruelty upon the saints of God and had defiled His Temple" (*Comm.* Ch.11, v.36).

Certain traits, Jerome explains, such as pretense of chastity, idolatry, and deceitful rewards, better fit the Antichrist than Antiochus. "The next statement, 'and he shall worship a god whom his fathers did not know' is more appropriate to the Antichrist than to Antiochus. . . . The Antichrist likewise is going to make lavish bestowal of many rewards upon those whom he has deceived, and will divide up the land to his soldiery" (*Comm.* Ch.11, v.37–39).

Jerome emphasizes the Antichrist's global ambition and eventual defeat, writing, "Those of our party . . . explain the final chapter of this vision as relating to the Antichrist, he shall come up to the summit . . . of the Mount of Olives, . . . and no one shall be able to assist the Antichrist as the Lord vents His fury upon him. Our school of thought insists that Antichrist is going to perish in that spot from which the Lord ascended to heaven" (*Comm.* Ch.11, v.44–45).

In contrast to Porphyry's historical reading, Jerome shows the prophetic depth of Daniel. Scripture often conveys ultimate truths through historical types. Antiochus's persecution foreshadows the Antichrist's opposition to God, culminating in divine judgment. The passage invites believers to trust in Christ's victory, foreseen even in the midst of history's trials, and to recognize that all false powers ultimately fall before the kingdom of the Son of Man.

MEDITATIO

Magnify and Exalt

Daniel prophesies of a king who "shall be lifted up, and shall magnify himself . . . and he shall speak great things against the God of gods" (Dan. 11:36), and "he shall fix his tabernacle . . . upon a glorious and holy mountain: and he shall come even to the top thereof" (Dan. 11:45). He seeks to exalt himself above God and others. Yet our Lord reminds us, "Whosoever shall exalt himself shall be humbled; he that shall humble himself shall be exalted" (Matt. 23:12).

If we seek the model of true humility, we need look no further than Our Lady: At the Annunciation, when Gabriel proclaims the coming Incarnation, she replies, "Behold the handmaid of the Lord; be it done to me according to thy word" (Luke 1:38). Literally, she calls herself δούλη, "the slave-girl of the Lord," humbling herself completely before God. Because of this radical humility, God exalts her. She receives the gift of glory beyond all measure, crowned with stars and clothed with the sun (Rev. 12:1). Her exaltation is not of her own merit, but a pure gift of God's grace.

Our natural desires often pull us toward self-exaltation, but Mary shows the way to true greatness: humble abandonment to God's will. At the Visitation, when Elizabeth praises her, she responds, "My soul doth magnify the Lord" (Luke 1:46). Mary reflects every praise back to God. She does not claim her own holiness; she mirrors God's grace, just as the moon reflects the sun's light.

Following Mary's path, we learn to magnify God instead of ourselves. The more we imitate her humility and openness to divine grace, the more our lives become instruments of God's glory. Every act of true humility, every surrender of self, draws us closer to the life of Christ and magnifies the Lord in the world around us.

ORATIO

1. In what areas of my life am I tempted to "magnify myself"? How can I instead choose humility as Mary did?

2. How can I more fully reflect God's grace in my words, actions, and relationships?

3. How can I practice magnifying the Lord in my daily life, especially when I am recognized or praised by others?

CONTEMPLATIO

LECTIO: DANIEL 12:1–4

SUBJECT: ST. MICHAEL, END OF DAYS

1 But at that time shall Michael rise up, the great prince, **who
standeth for the children of thy people**: and a time shall come
such as never was from the time that nations began even until that
time. **And at that time shall thy people be saved, every one that
shall be found written in the book.** 2 **And many of those that
sleep in the dust of the earth, shall awake: some unto life ever-
lasting, and others unto reproach, to see it always.** 3 **But they
that are learned shall shine as the brightness of the firmament:
and they that instruct many to justice, as stars for all eterni-
ty.** 4 But thou, O Daniel, shut up the words, and seal the book,
even to the time appointed: many shall pass over, and knowledge
shall be manifold.

READING WITH SAINT JEROME

In the beginning of Chapter 12, we are given both a historical and an eschatological vision of tribulation, judgment, and salvation. St. Jerome notes that Porphyry restricted this prophecy solely to the time of Antiochus, claiming that "the tribulation was such as had never previously occurred . . . even unto that time" (*Comm.* Ch.12, v.1–3). Jerome acknowledges the historical context—the suffering and later deliverance of those who remained faithful—writing that "the people of Israel experienced salvation, even all who had been written down in the book of God, that is, those who defended the law with great bravery. Contrasted with them were those who proved to be transgressors of the Law and sided with the party of Antiochus" (*Comm.* Ch.12, v.1–3).

However, Jerome firmly rejects Porphyry's claim that these events were merely symbolic. Instead, he insists, "the more reasonable understanding of the matter is that in the time of the Antichrist there shall occur a tribulation such as there has never been since nations began to exist" (*Comm.* Ch.12, v.1–3). After the Antichrist is destroyed, "the people written in God's book shall be saved; and in accordance with the merits of each, some shall rise up unto eternal life and others unto eternal shame" (*Comm.* Ch.12, v.1–3).

Daniel also affirms the glory prepared for those who teach and guide others in faithfulness. "The teachers shall resemble the very heavens . . . for it is not enough to know wisdom unless one also instructs others" (*Comm.* Ch.12, v.1–3).

Finally, Jerome explains that the mystery of Daniel's vision is divinely sealed. "He orders him to roll up the scroll . . . with the result that many shall read it and inquire as to its fulfilment in history" (*Comm.* Ch.12, v.4). He links this to the sealed scroll in Isaiah (Isa. 39:11) and the book with seven seals in Revelation (Rev. 5:4), which can be opened only by Christ, the one who fully unveils "the mysteries of Scripture . . . and its hidden truths" (*Comm.* Ch.12, v.4).

MEDITATIO

Daniel prophesies that in the end times when the Church is in her final battle, St. Michael the archangel will rise up to protect her. We see this reprised in the book of Revelation when Michael casts out Satan and his allies from heaven (Rev. 12:7). It is not possible for us to conceive of what this "great war" was like between the angels. But we know that Satan has brought this warfare down to earth and has harbored hatred against us from the beginning. He caused our first parents to fall because of his great hatred for God. He has continued this hatred throughout history and will continue it until the consummation of the world. The Church will never have complete peace in this world because her enemy constantly wages war on her children. But we have a great advocate who has already defeated him in the angelic plain. This is why we need to call constantly on St. Michael to "Defend us in battle" and to be "our protection against the wickedness and snares of the devil." We beg him to "cast into hell Satan and all evil spirits" so that the diabolic plans to separate us from God will be extinguished.

We need to ask for protection in our exterior battles and for the Church as a whole, but we also should pray that St. Michael will be victorious in our interior lives as well. The roots of sin and rebellion are deep within us. So, as we pray that Michael will slay the dragon, we ask him to slay the enemy within, too. This requires brutal honesty in our spiritual life. We must first admit that we have these unholy desires, and only when we show it to God can we ask St. Michael to slay the evil that remains in us. Cast out of our souls any influence from the enemy. This is even more important than any exterior battle we may fight.

The St. Michael Prayer

Pope Leo XIII had a mystical vision at the end of the nineteenth century in which he witnessed a conversation between Jesus and Satan. (Similar to a conversation that we find in the book of Job between God and Satan.) Satan boasted that all he would need was one hundred years to destroy the Church. The Lord gave him permission to try. It was during this vision that the pope was inspired to write the St. Michael Prayer. He then exhorted the whole Church to pray this prayer after every Mass, seeing that we would need extra help to stay aligned with God.

Even though more than a hundred years have passed, we are still in great need of this prayer and Michael's protection. We need to reclaim devotion to the archangel Michael who is the one in Revelation who casts out Satan from heaven (Rev. 12:7–9). We need him in our personal lives to cast Satan and his minions far from us.

The Prayer

St. Michael the Archangel,
defend us in battle.
Be our protection against the wickedness and snares of the devil;
may God rebuke him, we humbly pray;
and do thou, O Prince of the heavenly host,
by the power of God, cast into hell Satan
and all the evil spirits
who prowl about the world seeking the ruin of souls.
Amen.

ORATIO

1. Where in my life do I most need St. Michael's protection?

2. What habits, attachments, or patterns of thought in my life align more with the spirit of God, and which reflect the lingering influence of the enemy within me?

3. The St. Michael Prayer was given in a time of spiritual warfare for the Church. How seriously do I take the reality of this unseen battle, and what concrete change can I make to reclaim Michael's protection in my daily prayer life?

CONTEMPLATIO

LECTIO: DANIEL 12:5–10

Subject: Tribulation and Purification

5 And I Daniel looked, and behold as it were two others stood: one on this side upon the bank of the river, and another on that side, on the other bank of the river. 6 And I said to the man that was clothed in linen, that stood upon the waters of the river: How long shall it be to the end of these wonders? 7 And I heard the man that was clothed in linen, that stood upon the waters of the river: when he had lifted up his right hand, and his left hand to heaven, and had sworn, by him that liveth for ever, that it should be unto a time, and times, and half a time. And when the scattering of the band of the holy people shall be accomplished, all these things shall be finished. 8 And I heard, and understood not. And I said: O my lord, what shall be after these things? 9 And he said: Go, Daniel, because the words are shut up, and sealed until the appointed time. **10 Many shall be chosen, and made white, and shall be tried as fire: and the wicked shall deal wickedly, and none of the wicked shall understand, but the learned shall understand.**

Reading with Saint Jerome

In Daniel's vision, two mysterious figures appear standing on opposite banks of a river, while a man clothed in linen stands upon the waters. Daniel, overwhelmed by what he has seen, asks how long it will be until these wonders are fulfilled. Lifting both hands toward heaven, the man swears by the eternal God that it will be "unto a time, and times, and half a time" and that all will be accomplished when "the scattering of the band of the holy people" is complete.

St. Jerome identifies the setting of this vision, writing, "Daniel saw two angels standing on either side upon the bank of the river of Babylon. Although it is mentioned here without specifying its name, I suppose that . . . it would be the Tigris River" (*Comm.* Ch.12, v.5–6). Of the angel who speaks, Jerome says, "But this first angel was the gracious one who had presented Daniel's prayers before God during the twenty-one days" (*Comm.* Ch.12, v.5–6). Daniel, he explains, "was asking him about these wonders spoken of in the present vision, as to the time when they should be accomplished" (*Comm.* Ch.12, v.5–6).

Jerome contrasts pagan and Christian interpretation, writing, "Porphyry . . . assigns this time to the period of Antiochus . . . whereas we assign it to the time of Antichrist" (*Comm.* Ch.12, v.5–6). While acknowledging that "a time and times and half a time" corresponds to three and a half years, Jerome ties it to the final persecution, when "the people of God shall have been scattered . . . either under the persecution of Antiochus . . . or of Antichrist, which we deem to be closer to fact" (*Comm.* Ch.12, v.7).

Though Daniel longs to understand, the words are sealed. As Jerome writes, "The prophet wished to comprehend what he had seen . . . and he desired to understand the reality of the things to come" (*Comm.* Ch.12, v.8–10). Yet "when the end comes, the ungodly will lack comprehension, whereas those who are learned in the teaching of God will be able to understand. 'For wisdom will not enter the perverted soul'" (*Comm.* Ch.12, v.10).

This passage reminds us that tribulation purifies the just, confusion blinds the wicked, and only those formed by God's wisdom are able to discern His purposes in times of trial.

MEDITATIO

The Church's Ultimate Trial

In this prophecy of Daniel, we get a faint foreshadowing of the Church in the end times. Because Our Lord has promised that the gates of hell will not prevail over His Church, we may think the end times will see the Church rise up in triumphant glory above all earthly powers like a final blossoming of victorious Christendom. But this could not be further from the truth. The Church will indeed be triumphant, but her way will be none other than her Lord's way to glory, and this is the way of the cross. As the *Catechism* states:

"Before Christ's second coming the Church must pass through a final trial that will shake the faith of many believers" (*CCC* 675). And, "The persecution that accompanies her pilgrimage on earth will unveil the 'mystery of iniquity'" (*CCC* 675). While elsewhere stating: "The Church will enter the glory of the kingdom only through this final Passover, when she will follow her Lord in his death and Resurrection. The kingdom will be fulfilled, then, not by a historic triumph of the Church through a progressive ascendancy, but only by God's victory over the final unleashing of evil, which will cause his Bride to come down from heaven" (*CCC* 677).

This means that the Church as a whole will experience some sort of grand crucifixion at the end of time. We have no concept of what this could possibly look like. But we get glimpses here in Daniel. It says the holy ones will experience a definitive *scattering* (Dan. 12:7). The members of the Church will experience a dispersion that will bring isolation from support. Could this involve loss of sacraments? No access to Mass or the Eucharist? In 2020, the Church as a whole got a small glimpse of what something like this could be as the Covid-19 pandemic swept the globe.

They will be tried in *fire*, the angel says (Dan. 12:10). This could come as physical suffering or torture, but could it also be a psychological or reputational fire? Has the Church not experienced this kind of fire in the past decades? Our Lord Himself was accused of blasphemy and His reputation was completely destroyed during His passion.

And the children of the Church will be made *white* (Dan. 12:10). The Book of Revelation says that the saints will be made white in the blood of the lamb. This means there will be some kind of mass persecution in which martyrs will be so abundant that they are beyond counting. This is not well known, but there were more martyrs in the twentieth century than in all previous centuries combined. Is this not a participation in the Lord's passion?

If we want to know what the Church's passion will look like, then we need to study our Lord's passion in detail. It will look the same as His because the Church is the mystical Body of Christ, and her passion is nothing other than His passion. Where the Head has gone, the Body must follow. She will be abandoned like Him. She will be hated and spat upon like Him. Her blood will spill immodestly on the ground just like His. Jesus was abandoned by the Church on the cross. Yes, the Church led by Peter abandoned Him. The priesthood which He had just established hours before abandoned Him, except for one priest, John, standing at the foot of His cross.

The Church should expect all the aspects of Christ's suffering to come upon her at the end. And although the Church's definitive entrance into the passion will not come until the end of the world, we experience some of it now. We should not just see this as some distant event. The Church already and in every age experiences different elements of the passion.

When we experience suffering, and especially injustice, it is our opportunity to unite ourselves to Jesus on the cross. None of us are innocent, at best we can hope to be like the good thief. He knew that his suffering was deserved but begged Jesus for mercy. This is where we are when we suffer. We are hanging with Jesus on the cross. We can either curse God like the bad thief, or pray to him for mercy like the good thief. Suffering is the hammer that unites us to Jesus. We have always had a suspicion that the cross would come one way or another even though we tried to ignore it. But now it is here. There is nowhere to go. Someone will stretch out our hands and lead us where we do not want to go (John 21). And now it is our turn to pray, "Lord, remember me when thou shalt come into thy kingdom" (Luke 23:42).

ORATIO

1. How do I respond to my own "scattering"? Do I cling more tightly to Christ when I feel isolated, confused, or unsupported?

2. When I am "tried by fire" through suffering, misunderstanding, or injustice, do I unite myself to Christ on the Cross, or resist the purification He offers me?

3. In the face of the Church's present struggles, am I growing deeper in faith and repentance like the good thief, or am I tempted to doubt and withdraw?

CONTEMPLATIO

LECTIO: DANIEL 12:11–13

Subject: Endurance of Hope

11 And from the time when the continual sacrifice shall be taken
away, and the abomination unto desolation shall be set up, there
shall be a **thousand two hundred ninety days,** 12 **Blessed is he
that waiteth and cometh unto a thousand three hundred thir-
ty-five days.** 13 But **go thou thy ways until the time appointed:**
and thou shalt rest, and stand in thy lot unto the end of the days.

Reading with Saint Jerome

This passage shifts our gaze from historical persecution to the final trial of the Church and the resurrection of the dead. While some commentators, such as Porphyry, confined this prophecy to the desecration of the Temple under Antiochus, St. Jerome rejects this reduction. He notes, "Porphyry asserts that these one thousand two hundred and ninety days were fulfilled in the desolation of the Temple in the time of Antiochus . . . From this circumstance it is apparent that the three and a half years are spoken of in connection with the time of the Antichrist, for he is going to persecute the saints for three and a half years" (*Comm.* Ch.12, v.11). Thus, Jerome sees in Daniel's numbers a prefigurement of the Antichrist's final assault against the worship of God.

Jerome continues, "From the time of the removal of the continual sacrifice . . . the time when the Antichrist shall obtain possession of the world . . . and forbid the worship of God, unto the day of his death the three and a half years shall be fulfilled" (*Comm.* Ch.12, v.11). Yet those who endure beyond this period are called blessed. "He is blessed who waits for forty-five days . . . for it is within that period that our Lord and Savior is to come in His glory" (*Comm.* Ch.12, v.12). The precise reason for these additional days remains hidden within God's providence, perhaps a final testing of perseverance.

Finally, when Daniel is told he will "rest" and "stand in his lot," Jerome affirms, "the whole context of the prophecy has to do with the resurrection of all the dead, at the time when the prophet also is to rise" (*Comm.* Ch.12, v.13). Thus, the message ends not in fear, but in hope. Faithful endurance leads to resurrection and glory.

MEDITATIO

Blessed is He that Waits

This might sound strange to us: "Blessed is he that waiteth." Why should waiting be blessed? It is such an ordinary experience—something we all do every day—yet Scripture clearly presents it as a virtue. The Psalms are filled with prayers of waiting (cf. Ps. 27, 33, 37; Prov. 20:20). But why is waiting so highly exalted? Simply put, because we are terrible at it.

Consider a child: he wants what he wants when he wants it, and if he does not get it, he can be inconsolable. He does not really know what is good for him. That is the parent's task—to guide his desires and sometimes deny what he asks for in order to give what he truly needs. Instead of ice cream for breakfast, perhaps eggs. The analogy quickly becomes clear: we are God's children. But the difference between our understanding and His wisdom is infinitely greater than that between a child and a parent. God does not have to guess. He knows precisely what we need.

Waiting is one of the primary means God uses to bring our wills into order and train us in hope. In Daniel 12, the man who waits until one thousand three hundred and thirty-five days is called blessed, though the affliction itself lasts only one thousand two hundred and ninety days. This is not mere ordinary waiting, but waiting on the Lord—hope that outlasts suffering.

What is being described here is not simple optimism, but the theological virtue of hope, which infused into our souls at baptism. Like a muscle, it must be exercised if it is to grow. Waiting is how God strengthens it.

Too often we are like infants, restless and demanding. But as a wise parent waits for a storm to pass, so God waits for us, and in doing so, teaches us how to wait for Him.

ORATIO

1. Where in my life is God asking me to wait right now? Am I responding with trustful hope, or with frustration and impatience?

2. In what ways do I act more like a child demanding immediate satisfaction, and how might God be using denial or delay to form in me the virtue of supernatural hope?

3. Do I truly believe that God knows what I need better than I do? What practical change would happen in my prayer and decisions if I surrendered my timeline more fully to His wisdom?

CONTEMPLATIO

LECTIO: DANIEL 13:1–11

Subject: Inner Beauty, Purity of Heart

1 Now there was a man that dwelt in Babylon, and his name was Joakim: 2 And he took a wife whose name was Susanna, the daughter of Helcias, a very beautiful woman, and one that feared God. 3 For her parents being just, had instructed their daughter according to the law of Moses. 4 Now Joakim was very rich, and had an orchard near his house: and the Jews resorted to him, because he was the most honourable of them all. 5 **And there were two of the ancients of the people appointed judges that year, of whom the Lord said: Iniquity came out from Babylon from the ancient judges, that seemed to govern the people.** 6 **These men frequented the house of Joakim, and all that had any matters of judgment came to them.** 7 **And when the people departed away at noon, Susanna went in, and walked in her husband's orchard.** 8 **And the old men saw her going in every day, and walking: and they were inflamed with lust towards her:** 9 And they perverted their own mind and turned away their eyes that they might not look unto heaven, nor remember just judgments. 10 So they were both wounded with the love of her, yet they did not make known their grief one to the other: 11 For they were ashamed to declare to one another their lust, being desirous to have to do with her.

Reading with Saint Jerome

Daniel introduces Susanna as a woman formed in virtue, "instructed . . . according to the law of Moses," and as one who "feared God" (Dan. 13:2–3). Her holiness is placed in deliberate contrast with the corruption of the two elders appointed as judges. Though invested with authority, their leadership is only an appearance, as St. Jerome explains: "Very appropriately it is not said of these sinful elders, 'They governed the people,' but rather, 'They appeared to govern.' . . . Those who merely have the title of judge and lead the people unjustly only appear to govern" (*Comm.* Ch.13, v.5). This passage reveals how spiritual and moral authority can be hollowed out by sin while retaining an exterior respectability.

Their fall begins in the interior life. Seeing Susanna, they "were inflamed with lust," and Jerome clarifies the nature of this descent: "What the Greeks call pathos we render more correctly by 'emotion' than by 'passion.' And so it was this emotion, this lustful desire, which aroused or even smote the hearts of the elders" (*Comm.* Ch.13, v.8). Instead of resisting, "they perverted their own minds" (*Comm.* Ch. 13, v.8), severing themselves from God. As their interior vision darkened, so did their spiritual perception: "they turned away their eyes that they might not regard heavenly things or remember righteous judgments, or God, or honor, or character" (*Comm.* Ch.13, v.8).

This movement from lust to blindness illustrates how sin begins in the heart, distorts reason, and ultimately corrupts justice itself.

MEDITATIO

Susanna is described as "very beautiful" and as a woman who "feared God." There is nothing sinful about beauty. In fact, earthly beauty is a reflection of divine beauty. But physical beauty alone is not something we earn. It is received, not achieved. It is a gift of God, given through nature and inheritance. What truly reveals the soul, however, is interior beauty—the hidden harmony of a heart aligned with God.

Susanna's true beauty came from the fact that she "feared God" and was "just" according to the law of Moses. In Scripture, to be just is not simply to obey rules externally but to be inwardly ordered to God. Not outward conformity, but a heart shaped by love for Him. This is precisely what Christ calls us to in the Gospel: a transformed heart.

The two elders demonstrate the opposite path. "They were inflamed with lust towards her . . . and turned away their eyes that they might not look unto heaven" (Dan. 13:8–9). Their sin began within. Lust is not love, but a distortion of love—a desire to use rather than to give. As Karol Wojtyła—later Pope St. John Paul II—teaches in Love and Responsibility, the opposite of love is not hate, but *use*. No human person is meant to be used.

Custody of the eyes is therefore not a judgment against another's beauty, but an act of humility about my own woundedness. I look away, not because the other is the problem, but because my heart needs healing. The remedy is to do the opposite of the elders: not to turn my eyes from heaven, but to lift them toward it. In grace, desire can be purified and love restored.

ORATIO

1. Is my concern for outward appearance greater than my desire for interior holiness? What concrete steps am I taking to become more "just" and God-fearing in my heart?

2. Where do I see disordered desire or the temptation to "use" others in my thoughts, imagination, or behaviors? How am I inviting Christ to purify those desires?

3. In moments of temptation, do I turn my eyes away from God like the elders, or do I intentionally lift my mind and heart toward heaven in prayer and self-control?

CONTEMPLATIO

LECTIO: DANIEL 13:12–21

Subject: Corruption of Heart

12 **And they watched carefully every day to see her.** And one said
to the other: 13 Let us now go home, for it is dinner time. So going
out they departed one from another. 14 And turning back again,
they came both to the same place: and asking one another the
cause, they acknowledged their lust; and then they agreed upon
a time, when they might find her alone. 15 And it fell out, as they
watched a fit day, she went in on a time, as yesterday and the day
before, with two maids only, and was desirous to wash herself in
the orchard: for it was hot weather. 16 And there was nobody there,
but the two old men that had hid themselves and were beholding
her. 17 So she said to the maids: Bring me oil, and washing balls,
and shut the doors of the orchard, that I may wash me. 18 And
they did as she bade them: and they shut the doors of the orchard,
and went out by a back door to fetch what she had commanded
them, and they knew not that the elders were hid within. 19 **Now**
when the maids were gone forth, the two elders arose, and ran
to her, and said: 20 **Behold the doors of the orchard are shut,**
and nobody seeth us, and we are in love with thee: wherefore
consent to us, and lie with us. 21 **But if thou wilt not, we will**
bear witness against thee, that a young man was with thee, and
therefore thou didst send away thy maids from thee.

Reading with Saint Jerome

In this passage, the corruption of the two elders moves from hidden desire to deliberate conspiracy. They no longer merely "burn with lust"; they now plan in coordination, watching Susanna's habits and waiting for a moment when she is most vulnerable. Sin, when entertained, always seeks opportunity. What began in the imagination now advances into calculated action.

Susanna, meanwhile, appears in her simplicity and modesty. Her desire to wash is entirely innocent, and the presence of the maids affirms her concern for propriety. The elders exploit the moment when she is alone and use the closed garden not as a place of beauty, but as a cover for sin. Their words reveal the full violence of lust: "consent to us, and lie with us." When she refuses, they move to blackmail, attempting to destroy her reputation by false accusation. Lust matures into cruelty.

Saint Jerome, however, reminds us of both human weakness and virtue. "Anyone who has attained to the acme of perfect virtue never says that she is faced with a crisis of decision…." (*Comm.* Ch.13, v.19). Yet he also acknowledges the reality of fear: "It is of course a characteristic of human frailty to fear a death which is inflicted upon one because of his uprightness." Susanna's distress, then, does not signify moral weakness, but the natural fear of suffering and disgrace: "the contumely and disgrace which would be heaped upon her by those accusers" (*Comm.* Ch.13, v.19).

This scene reveals the deep opposition between innocence and corruption, and prepares us for God's defense of the just.

MEDITATIO

These old men made worse choices the deeper they went. Each had already indulged lustful thoughts and desires, but when they came across one another in the garden, they were given an unexpected opportunity for grace. They could have confessed their sins to one another and encouraged each other toward virtue. Instead, they found a kind of corrupt companionship in their shared shame.

Rather than recognizing their covetousness toward their neighbor's wife and taking decisive action to curb it, they fed it. They watched her day after day, intentionally cultivating lust in their hearts. When their sin finally came into the light, instead of repenting, they conspired together to commit an even greater evil against Susanna. It is difficult to imagine a more tragic hardening of the heart.

But we must be careful not to linger too long in judgment of these wicked elders alone. The roots of their sin are present in every human heart. If we do not first acknowledge our desire to use others for our own satisfaction, and then discipline those desires through prayer, fasting, custody of the senses, and the pursuit of virtue, those same disordered inclinations can grow into full-blown mortal sin. This is why the Church so strongly warns us about the near occasion of sin.

It is difficult to exaggerate how important it is to turn away from the occasion of sin as soon as it presents itself. In that moment, two voices speak within us: One gently urges us to turn away, to choose the path of God, to flee while we still can. The other reassures us that "it's no big deal," that an occasion of sin is not actually sin, that we can take a small taste without giving ourselves over entirely. This second voice is subtle and persuasive. But if we allow the fire to burn even a little longer, it will quickly grow beyond our control. We must learn to recognize the first, gentle voice and respond immediately, choosing God while our freedom is still strong. As *The Imitation of Christ* wisely warns:

> "Above all, we must be especially alert against the beginnings of temptation, for the enemy is more easily conquered if he is refused admittance to the mind and is met beyond the threshold when he knocks. Someone has said very aptly: 'Resist the beginnings; remedies come too late, when by long delay the evil has gained strength.' First, a mere thought comes to mind, then strong imagination, followed by pleasure, evil delight, and consent. Thus, because he is not resisted in the beginning, Satan gains full entry. And the longer a man delays in resisting, so much the weaker does he become each day, while the strength of the enemy grows against him'" (Book I, Chapter 13)

We must therefore cultivate the habit of recognizing the occasion of sin the moment it appears and turning from it without hesitation. This vigilance is not fear—it is love. It is one of the surest ways to remain in the state of grace and to guard the purity of the heart God desires for us.

ORATIO

1. Where in my daily life do I repeatedly place myself in the near occasion of sin? What can I do this week to remove or avoid that situation?

2. When I feel temptation rising, how can I better avoid the voice of sin and cling tighter to the voice that calls me back to God?

3. What spiritual practices (prayer, fasting, frequent confession) do I need to strengthen so that disordered desires do not take root and grow in my heart?

CONTEMPLATIO

LECTIO: DANIEL 13:22–41

Subject: Death Rather than Sin

22 Susanna sighed, and said: I am straitened on every side: for if I do this thing, it is death to me: and if I do it not, I shall not escape your hands. 23 But it is better for me to fall into your hands without doing it, than to sin in the sight of the Lord. 24 With that Susanna cried out with a loud voice: and the elders also cried out against her. 25 And one of them ran to the door of the orchard, and opened it. 26 So when the servants of the house heard the cry in the orchard, they rushed in by the back door to see what was the matter. 27 But after the old men had spoken, the servants were greatly ashamed: for never had there been any such word said of Susanna. And on the next day, 28 When the people were come to Joakim her husband, the two elders also came full of wicked device against Susanna, to put her to death. 29 And they said before the people: Send to Susanna daughter of Helcias the wife of Joakim. And presently they sent. 30 And she came with her parents, and children, and all her kindred. 31 Now Susanna was exceeding delicate, and beautiful to behold. 32 But those wicked men commanded that her face should be uncovered, (for she was covered,) that so at least they might be satisfied with her beauty. 33 Therefore her friends and all her acquaintance wept. 34 But the two elders rising up in the midst of the people, laid their hands upon her head. 35 And she weeping looked up to heaven, for her heart had confidence in the Lord. 36 And the elders said: As we walked in the orchard alone, this woman came in with two maids, and shut the doors of the orchard, and sent away the maids from her. 37 Then a young man that was there hid came to her, and lay with her. 38 But we that were in a corner of the orchard, seeing this wickedness, ran up to them, and we saw them lie together. 39 And him indeed we could not take, because he was stronger than us, and opening the doors he leaped out: 40 But having taken this woman, we asked who the young man was, but she would not tell us: of this thing we are witnesses. 41 The multitude believed them as being the elders and the judges of the people, and they condemned her to death.

Reading with Saint Jerome

Susanna finds herself "straitened on every side," yet in that moment of terror, her conscience is clear: better to suffer death at the hands of men than to sin before God (Dan. 13:23). Her choice reveals a properly ordered soul—one that fears sin more than suffering. As Saint Jerome writes, "She speaks of sin as death. For just as in the case of one who commits adultery, the adultery means death, so also every sin which results in death is to be equated with death. And we believe we die as often as we sin unto death. And therefore on the other hand we rise again and are made alive just as often as we perform deeds which are worthy of life" (*Comm.* Ch.13, v.22). Susanna's refusal is an act of spiritual life in the face of physical danger.

When she cries out, her voice is not powerful by force, but by purity. Jerome notes, "Her voice was great, not because of the intense vibrations it sent through the air nor because of the outcry that came from her lips, but because of the greatness of the chastity with which she called out to the Lord" (*Comm.* Ch.13, v.24). The elders also cry out, but their voices carry no such strength, for Scripture simply says, "The elders also cried out against her" (Dan. 13:24), (*Comm.* Ch.13, v.24).

Though the people believe the false judgment of respected men, Susanna remains rooted in trust. Her gaze lifted to God reveals the heart of sanctity: fidelity even when the world condemns, and confidence that the Lord sees and will judge justly.

MEDITATIO

Saint Dominic Savio one stated, "Death rather than sin." Susanna presents this same conviction, acting in the exact opposite manner of the wicked elders. Trapped and on the verge of rape, she recognizes that sin is worse than death. Her heart is aligned with God's law, and she responds immediately: better to die than to offend God (Dan. 13:23). Unlike the elders, who cultivated lust in their minds and fell quickly into temptation, Susanna's virtue is solid. She does not hesitate, and her decision comes from a soul steeped in prayer and familiarity with the Lord. St. Maria Goretti mirrors Susanna in our own day: confronted with sexual violence, she refused sin even at the cost of her life.

This swift fidelity to God requires a deep spiritual life. If we cultivate intimacy with Christ, we, too, can recognize occasions of sin and respond decisively. As Jesus teaches, we must pray, "Lead us not into temptation, but deliver us from evil" (Matt. 6:13).

The elders' act of laying hands on Susanna's head (Dan 13:34) carries a dark symbolism. They make her a scapegoat for their sins, echoing the Day of Atonement ritual in which the high priest lays hands on a goat to transfer sins (Lev. 16:20). This warns us against calumny and detraction, sins that damage the reputation of others (*CCC* 2477–79). Today, social media amplifies our ability to scapegoat others. When we witness wrongdoing, instead of joining in condemnation, we should pray for the person and examine our own hearts, confessing our sins to God.

Susanna teaches us that fidelity to God, immediate rejection of sin, and the protection of others' reputations are inseparable marks of a virtuous life.

ORATIO

1. Do I respond quickly to grace, or do I hesitate when faced with temptation?

2. When I witness the faults or failings of others, do I ever participate in calumny or detraction, even indirectly, through words or social media? How can I choose prayer and mercy instead?

3. In what areas of my life am I tempted to shift blame or make others bear the consequences of my sins? How can I take responsibility for my actions and turn instead to God in repentance?

CONTEMPLATIO

LECTIO: DANIEL 13:42–65

Subject: Innocent Blood is Not Spared

[42] Then Susanna cried out with a loud voice, and said: O eternal God, who knowest hidden things, who knowest all things before they come to pass, [43] Thou knowest that they have borne false witness against me: and behold I must die, whereas I have done none of these things, which these men have maliciously forged against me. [44] And the Lord heard her voice. [45] And when she was led to be put to death, the Lord raised up the holy spirit of a young boy, whose name was Daniel. [46] And he cried out with a loud voice I am clear from the blood of this woman. [47] Then all the people turning themselves towards him, said: What meaneth this word that thou hast spoken? [48] But he standing in the midst of them, said: Are ye so foolish, ye children of Israel, that without examination or knowledge of the truth, you have condemned a daughter of Israel? [49] Return to judgment, for they have borne false witness against her. [50] So all the people turned again in haste, and the old men said to him: Come, and sit thou down among us, and shew it us: seeing God hath given thee the honour of old age. [51] And Daniel said to the people: Separate these two far from one another, and I will examine them. [52] So when they were put asunder one from the other, he called one of them, and said to him: O thou that art grown old in evil days, now are thy sins come out, which thou hast committed before: [53] In judging unjust judgments, oppressing the innocent, and letting the guilty to go free, whereas the Lord saith: The innocent and the just thou shalt not kill. [54] Now then, if thou sawest her, tell me under what tree thou sawest them conversing together. He said: Under a mastic tree. [55] And Daniel said: Well hast thou lied against thy own head: for behold the angel of God having received the sentence of him, shall cut thee in two. [56] And having put him aside, he commanded that the other should come, and he said to him: O thou seed of Chanaan, and not of Juda, beauty hath deceived thee, and lust hath perverted thy heart: [57] Thus did you do to the daughters of Israel, and they for fear conversed with you: but a daughter of Juda would not abide your wickedness. [58] Now therefore tell me, under what tree didst thou take them conversing together. And he answered: Under a holm tree. [59] And Daniel said to him: Well hast thou also lied against thy own head: for the angel of the Lord waiteth with a sword to cut thee in two, and to destroy you. [60] **With that all the assembly cried out with a loud voice, and they blessed God, who saveth them that trust in him.** [61] And they rose up against the two elders, (for Daniel had convicted them of false witness by their own mouth,) and they did to them as they had maliciously dealt against their neighbour, [62] To fulfill the law of Moses: and they put them to death, and innocent blood was saved in that day. [63] But Helcias and his wife praised God, for their daughter Susanna, with Joakim her husband, and all her kindred, because there was no dishonesty found in her. [64] And Daniel became great in the sight of the people from that day, and thenceforward. [65] And king Astyages was gathered to his fathers, and Cyrus the Persian received his kingdom.

Reading with Saint Jerome[3]

In this passage, Susanna cries out to God: "O eternal God, who knowest hidden things . . . Thou knowest that they have borne false witness against me" (Dan. 13:42–43). Jerome observes, "Her voice was rendered the clearer because of the emotion of her heart, the honest sincerity of her avowal, and the uprightness of her conscience" (*Comm.* Ch.13, v.42). Her prayer demonstrates the power of innocence aligned with virtue, for although men would not listen, her outcry to God was great.

God raises the young Daniel, whose heart already bears the Holy Spirit: "By this language it is shown that the Holy Spirit did not then enter into Daniel, but rather that He was already within him, and only because of the tenderness of his years He had remained inactive" (*Comm.* Ch.13, v.45). Inspired, Daniel exposes the falsehoods of the elders, leading the assembly to vindicate Susanna and punish the guilty, fulfilling the law of Moses (Dan. 13:61–62). Jerome notes, "Like true saints they praise God . . . not simply on the ground of Susanna's deliverance . . . but rather on the ground that no immorality was found in her" (*Comm.* Ch.13, v.63).

---

3 Jerome wrestles with the canonical status of Daniel 13 (the story of Susanna) because the Hebrew Scriptures omit it. He notes that Daniel's questioning of the elders includes a wordplay on the trees' names: one elder says the encounter occurred under the mastic tree (*skhinos*), the other under the holm tree (*prinos*). In Greek, these names allow a pun on "cleaving" or "cutting" (*scissio, sectio, serratio*), which cannot be reproduced in Hebrew. Jerome concludes that, since the story relies on Greek etymology, it likely originated in Greek rather than Hebrew. He adds, however, that if a Hebrew derivation for these wordplays could be demonstrated, the chapter could be accepted as canonical (*Comm.* Ch.13, v.54 ff.).

This story exemplifies God's providential justice and the efficacy of prayer, innocence, and fidelity to virtue. It reminds the faithful that God hears the cries of the innocent, raises up instruments to defend truth, and brings deliverance even when human judgment falters.

MEDITATIO

Innocent Blood is Not Spared

In the liturgy, the Church pairs the story of Susanna with the Gospel account of the woman caught in adultery (Jn. 8:1–11). In Daniel 13, an innocent woman is falsely accused of adultery, and Daniel, inspired by God, exposes the lies of the elders. Through his clever questioning, Susanna's innocence is proven, and innocent blood is spared.

In John 8, the circumstances are different. The woman is guilty; she was caught in the act of sin. Jesus confronts the crowd, saying, "He that is without sin among you, let him first cast a stone at her" (John 8:7). One by one, beginning with the elders, the accusers depart. Her sin is undeniable, yet no innocent blood is shed on her behalf. Instead, Christ Himself assumes the burden of justice. He becomes the Lamb of God, the true scapegoat, taking upon Himself the punishment she deserved. Innocent blood is not spared—because it is the only blood that can redeem humanity.

In both stories, God raises up His instruments to accomplish justice. He hears Susanna's cry and inspires Daniel to defend her. The Scripture emphasizes that Daniel's discernment is not mere cleverness; it is divine revelation. Jerome notes that the Holy Spirit was present in Daniel, guiding his words (*Comm.* Ch.13, v.45). Similarly, when Peter confesses Jesus as the Messiah, the Lord says, "Flesh and blood hath not revealed it to thee, but my Father who is in heaven" (Matt. 16:17). Daniel's heart was attuned to God, ready to receive this inspiration, showing that fidelity to God opens us to His guidance in moments of trial.

ORATIO

1. When faced with temptation or injustice, do I turn immediately to God for guidance? Or do I hesitate and try to handle things on my own?

2. How aware am I of the ways Christ takes the punishment for our sins? Does that awareness shape my response to sin and mercy in my own life?

3. In what areas of my life am I open to the promptings of the Holy Spirit? Where might I need to cultivate a heart more attuned to God's guidance?

CONTEMPLATIO

LECTIO: DANIEL 14:1–21

Subject: Bel, Idolatry

[1] **And Daniel was the king's guest, and was honoured above all his friends.** [2] **Now the Babylonians had an idol called Bel:** and there were spent upon him every day twelve great measures of fine flour, and forty sheep, and sixty vessels of wine. [3] The king also worshipped him, and went every day to adore him: but Daniel adored his God. And the king said to him: Why dost thou not adore Bel? [4] And he answered, and said to him: Because I do not worship idols made with hands, but the living God, that created heaven and earth, and hath power over all flesh. [5] And the king said to him: Doth not Bel seem to thee to be a living god? Seest thou not how much he eateth and drinketh every day? [6] Then Daniel smiled and said: O king, be not deceived: for this is but clay within, and brass without, neither hath he eaten at any time. [7] And the king being angry called for his priests, and said to them: If you tell me not, who it is that eateth up these expenses, you shall die. [8] But if you can shew that Bel eateth these things, Daniel shall die, because he hath blasphemed against Bel. And Daniel said to the king: Be it done according to thy word. [9] Now the priests of Bel were seventy, besides their wives, and little ones, and children. And the king went with Daniel into the temple of Bel. [10] And the priests of Bel said: Behold we go out: and do thou, O king, set on the meats, and make ready the wine, and shut the door fast, and seal it with thy own ring: [11] And when thou comest in the morning, if thou findest not that Bel hath eaten up all, we will suffer death, or else Daniel that hath lied against us. [12] And they little regarded it, because they had made under the table a secret entrance, and they always came in by it, and consumed those things. [13] So it came to pass after they were gone out, the king set the meats before Bel: and Daniel commanded his servants, and they brought ashes, and he sifted them all over the temple before the king: and going forth they shut the door, and having sealed it with the king's ring, they departed. [14] But the priests went in by night, according to their custom, with their wives and their children: and they ate and drank up all. [15] And the king arose early in the morning, and Daniel with him. [16] And the king said: Are the seals whole, Daniel? And he answered: They are whole, O king. [17] And as soon

as he had opened the door, the king looked upon the table, and
cried out with a loud voice: Great art thou, O Bel, and there is
not any deceit with thee. 18 And Daniel laughed: and he held the
king that he should not go in: and he said: Behold the pavement,
mark whose footsteps these are. 19 And the king said: I see the
footsteps of men, and women, and children. And the king was
angry. 20 Then he took the priests, and their wives, and their chil-
dren: and they shewed him the private doors by which they came
in, and consumed the things that were on the table. 21 The king
therefore put them to death, and delivered Bel into the power of
Daniel: who destroyed him, and his temple.

Reading with Saint Jerome

In Daniel 14, we see Daniel confronted with the Babylonian idol Bel, which receives daily offerings from the king and the people. Daniel boldly refuses to worship it, saying, "I worship nothing but the Lord my God, who created the heaven and the earth" (St. Cyprian, *Epistle* 55). This statement highlights the central truth of biblical faith: true worship belongs only to the living God. The narrative exposes the fraud behind idol worship: the priests secretly consume the offerings through hidden entrances, deceiving the king and people (Tertullian, *On Idolatry* I, IV). By sprinkling ashes to reveal footprints, Daniel demonstrates their deceit, bringing justice while preserving the honor of God.

Jerome comments on the "great voice" of the king exalting Bel, noting that this story does not appear in the Hebrew text of Daniel. He cautiously refrains from treating the chapter as definitively canonical, but allows that if its authenticity were established, a fuller theological commentary would be necessary (*Comm.* Ch.14).

The chapter, regardless of canonical status in Jerome's time, offers important instruction. Daniel's courage shows that fidelity to God requires discernment, courage, and wisdom, even when societal pressure or popular belief favors falsehood. Idolatry, as Justin Martyr observes (*Dialogue with Trypho* IX), is "vain, empty, and unprofitable," maintained by human artifice rather than divine power. Clement of Rome similarly warns that idols are incapable of service and only enslave those who worship them (*Recognitiones*, V.14).

For the Christian today, Daniel's example teaches the importance of resisting cultural pressures to compromise faith. True worship calls for vigilance, courage, and discernment, rooted in the knowledge that God alone is living, righteous, and worthy of devotion.

MEDITATIO

The Absurdity of Idolatry and the Need for True Worship

When the king tries to convince Daniel that Bel is a "living god" because he eats and drinks, Daniel simply smiles. The absurdity of worshiping a statue that cannot move, eat, or think is clear. It seems obvious to us—but this clarity can lull us into pride, thinking we could never fall into such folly.

Idolatry, however, is rarely so literal. Consider how some devote themselves to sports or entertainment. Every Sunday, fans invest hours preparing tailgates, cheering with every fiber of their being, and reliving the game all week. Their emotional life rises and falls with the fortunes of a team. In devotion, in time, and in energy, this can become a kind of worship. There is nothing inherently wrong with enjoying sports or hobbies, but when they claim the attention and allegiance meant for God, they become idols.

We are made for worship. God has built into us both the capacity and the need to adore, praise, and order our hearts toward Him. If we do not direct this energy to God, we will inevitably worship something else—our passions, possessions, or pleasures. Daniel's smile is a reminder of the absurdity of worshiping the wrong thing. Let us examine our own lives and ask: What do I truly give my heart to? If it is not God, it is as hollow—and as absurd—as the idol of Bel.

ORATIO

1. What are the "idols" in my life (things, habits, or passions) that take the attention, energy, or devotion meant for God?

2. How do I devote time, emotion, and energy to God compared to other pursuits, like entertainment, hobbies, or work?

3. In what ways can I redirect my heart and worship more fully toward God in my daily life, rather than allowing lesser things to become false objects of devotion?

CONTEMPLATIO

LECTIO: DANIEL 14:22–42

Subject: The Dragon, The Lions' Den

22 And there was a great dragon in that place, and the Babylonians worshipped him. 23 And the king said to Daniel: Behold thou canst not say now, that this is not a living god: adore him therefore. 24 And Daniel said: I adore the Lord my God: for he is the living God: but that is no living god. 25 But give me leave, O king, and I will kill this dragon without sword or club. And the king said: I give thee leave. 26 Then Daniel took pitch, and fat, and hair, and boiled them together: and he made lumps, and put them into the dragon's mouth, and the dragon burst asunder. And he said: Behold him whom you worshipped. 27 And when the Babylonians had heard this, they took great indignation: and being gathered together against the king, they said: The king is become a Jew. He hath destroyed Bel, he hath killed the dragon, and he hath put the priests to death. 28 And they came to the king, and said: Deliver us Daniel, or else we will destroy thee and thy house. 29 And the king saw that they pressed upon him violently: and being constrained by necessity he delivered Daniel to them. 30 And they cast him into the den of lions, and he was there six days. **31 And in the den there were seven lions, and they had given to them two carcasses every day, and two sheep: but then they were not given unto them, that they might devour Daniel.** 32 Now there was in Judea a prophet called Habacuc, and he had boiled pottage, and had broken bread in a bowl: and was going into the field, to carry it to the reapers. 33 And the angel of the Lord said to Habacuc: Carry the dinner which thou hast into Babylon to Daniel, who is in the lions' den. 34 And Habacuc said: Lord, I never saw Babylon, nor do I know the den. 35 And the angel of the Lord took him by the top of his head, and carried him by the hair of his head, and set him in Babylon over the den in the force of his spirit. 36 And Habacuc cried, saying: O Daniel, thou servant of God, take the dinner that God hath sent thee. 37 And Daniel said: Thou hast remembered me, O God, and thou hast not forsaken them that love thee. 38 And Daniel arose and ate. And the angel of the Lord presently set Habacuc again in his own place. **39 And upon the seventh day the king came to bewail Daniel: and he came to the den, and looked in, and behold Daniel was sitting**

in the midst of the lions. [40] And the king cried out with a loud
voice, saying: Great art thou, O Lord the God of Daniel. And
he drew him out of the lions' den. [41] But those that had been
the cause of his destruction, he cast into the den, and they were
devoured in a moment before him. [42] Then the king said: Let
all the inhabitants of the whole earth fear the God of Daniel:
for he is the Saviour, working signs, and wonders in the earth:
who hath delivered Daniel out of the lions' den.

Reading with Saint Jerome

In the final verses of Daniel, we encounter the account of the great dragon worshiped by the Babylonians and Daniel's miraculous deliverance from the lions' den. The passage highlights the absurdity of idolatry, the reality of spiritual evil, and the power of God over all creation. When Daniel declares, "I adore the Lord my God: for he is the living God; but that is no living god" (Dan. 14:24), he reaffirms the truth that all idol worship is futile. The dragon represents false gods and, more broadly, the devil's deceit, as St. Victorinus notes: "From the beginning . . . he was a murderer; and he has oppressed the whole of the human race" (Commentary on the Apocalypse 12:3). By destroying the dragon without force, Daniel demonstrates God's supremacy over even the most feared and venerated powers.

Daniel's survival in the lions' den illustrates God's providential protection. The angelic intervention through Habacuc shows God's care not only for the faithful, but also for His instruments, guiding them to perform His will. St. Augustine observes, "Thus, because Daniel acknowledged God above him, the lions acknowledged him above them" (Homily VIII on 1 John), emphasizing that fear of the Lord places one above all threats. The lions, symbols of anger, lust, and worldly danger, could not harm Daniel because he trusted in God. St. Gregory Nazianzus similarly writes, "Fear the Lord, and it shall not be able to hurt you. 'A lion is blood-thirsty.' Fear the Lord and it shall lie down beside you, as by Daniel" (Oration 5).

This passage also invites reflection on the ordering of our desires. St. Maximus the Confessor explains that passions like gluttony, avarice, and self-esteem originate in self-love, and St. John Cassian shows how virtues counter each vice through prayer, self-control, and compassion. Daniel exemplifies mastery over passion through divine reliance, modeling how faithful alignment with God transforms danger into deliverance.

Ultimately, Daniel 14:22-42 teaches that idols and evil powers are powerless before the living God. Fear of the Lord, trust in divine providence, and the cultivation of virtue allow the faithful to face threats boldly. Just as Daniel's faith subdued the lions, so too can God's faithful overcome the trials and passions that assail the human heart.

MEDITATIO

The Dragon

After Daniel exposes the absurdity of worshiping Bel, the king presents a dragon, calling it a "living god" worthy of veneration. While some modern scholars see this as symbolic, many ancient authors understood the dragon as an actual creature. Bel, meaning "lord," likely refers to the Babylonian god Marduk, often associated with dragons. The dragon itself may have been a large serpent, lizard, or crocodile, all animals worshiped in the ancient Near East. Both Babylonians and Egyptians sometimes kept such creatures in sacred spaces, seeing them as symbols or manifestations of divinity.

Daniel's response is laughter. If it is absurd to worship a statue, it is even more ridiculous to worship a living reptile. By feeding the dragon a mixture that causes it to burst, Daniel demonstrates the obvious truth: animals are creatures, not gods. Beyond the literal, the dragon symbolizes the devil, the ancient serpent. Sin, like the dragon consuming itself, is seductive, yet destructive. Venial sins may seem small, but they deaden the conscience, making greater sins easier. Prayer, Eucharistic devotion, and frequent Confession help guard the soul from this slow self-destruction.

The Lion's Den and the Communion of Saints

In a remarkable turn, the angel of the Lord brings Habacuc to feed Daniel. Whether literal, bilocation, or mystical vision, the event reveals a profound truth: God uses the communion of saints to provide for one member through another. As the Catechism teaches, "None of us lives to himself, and none of us dies to himself. . . . Now you are the body of Christ and individually members of it" (*CCC* 953). Spiritual goods flow among the faithful—living, dead, and triumphant—through charity and prayer (*CCC* 955, 961). Habacuc did not know Babylon, yet God provided him with grace and wisdom. Likewise, the prayers of cloistered religious or distant believers may reach us without our knowledge. We are never truly alone; the Mystical Body of Christ binds all together in God's providence, reminding us that every act of charity, every prayer, contributes to the good of the whole Church.

ORATIO

1. In what ways might we unknowingly "worship" created things—entertainment, achievements, or comfort—rather than God? How can we reorient our hearts toward true worship?

2. How does the image of sin as a self-consuming dragon help you recognize the danger of venial sins and the importance of regular prayer, confession, and Eucharistic devotion?

3. How does the story of Habacuc feeding Daniel illustrate the reality of the communion of saints, and how might we more intentionally participate in this spiritual solidarity through prayer and acts of charity?

CONTEMPLATIO